W9-CER-133

DATE DUE

J

15

F

Homelessness

Look for these and other books in the Lucent Overview Series:

Abortion
Adoption
Alcoholism
Child Abuse
Children's Rights
Cities
Democracy
Drug Abuse
Family Violence
Gangs
Garbage
Homeless Children

Illegal Immigration
Illiteracy
Immigration
Juvenile Crime
Pesticides
Police Brutality
Population
Poverty
Recycling
Schools
World Hunger

Homelessness

by Sara Dixon Criswell

LUCENT BOOKS

LUCENT *Overview Series*

LUCENT *Overview Series*

Library of Congress Cataloging-in-Publication Data

Criswell, Sara Dixon, 1945–
    Homelessness / by Sara Dixon Criswell.
        p.   cm. — (Lucent overview series)
    Includes bibliographical references and index.
    Summary: Discusses the causes of homelessness, life on
the streets, homeless children, the shelter system, and help for the
homeless.
    ISBN 1-56006-180-4 (lib. : alk. paper)
    1. Homelessness—United States—Juvenile literature. 2.
Homeless persons—United States—Juvenile literature. [1.
Homelessness. 2. Homeless persons.]   I. Title.   II. Series.
HV4505.C75   1998
362.5'0973—dc21   97-42439
                                                                              CIP
                                                                              AC

Copyright © 1998 by Lucent Books, Inc.
P.O. Box 289011, San Diego, CA 92198-9011
Printed in the U.S.A.

Contents

Introduction

THROUGHOUT AMERICA'S HISTORY, people with no fixed address have been admired, scorned, respected, ridiculed, aided, and ignored. Books and motion pictures often portray cowboys, explorers, and drifters as American heroes. Popular songs glorify hoboes as "kings of the road." A fictitious child who runs away with a circus, or travels downriver on a raft, is viewed as an adventurer who leads a glamorous life of independence and freedom. People labeled as vagrants, tramps, and delinquents, however, receive no such glory on screen or on the street.

During colonial times, respected male artisans roamed from village to farm, securing work and lodging by knocking on doors. Settlers provided shelter in exchange for an artisan's services. Teachers without homes lived in the households of their students. Unskilled immigrants relied on workhouses, shelters, and soup kitchens in seaboard cities such as Boston and New York.

After railroads linked the east and west coasts in the 1860s, self-supporting hoboes "rode the rails" from one work site to another. In winter they lived in rooming houses where they paid their way with summer earnings. Their city neighborhoods were vibrant and healthy. Hoboes were proud of their self-sufficient lifestyle and were respected by other Americans as well.

When America's economy declined in the 1930s, during a time known worldwide as the Great Depression, 1.5 million American citizens suddenly had no home and no job. They depended on charity. Their pride suffered. Many men settled in shabby neighborhoods that became known as Skid Row. Affluent and more fortunate people labeled these men "Skid Row bums." Even after the economy improved, Skid Row lived on. The day of the hardworking hobo was gone forever. No one respected a bum.

During the 1960s many Skid Row neighborhoods were demolished to make way for new offices and upscale apartments. As affordable lodging places diminished, the poor took shelter in shacks and abandoned buildings where privacy made them invisible to their fellow citizens.

Although people without homes have always been present in America, it was not until the early 1980s that they received a new name. A small group of activists led by

A homeless man and his dog sleep in the doorway of an abandoned building.

Mitch Snyder and Robert Hayes named these people "the homeless." This new term has captured the attention of politicians, journalists, activists, and the American public.

As Snyder and Hayes pointed out, the homeless community changed in the 1980s. The homeless were no longer primarily older men nor were they confined to the inner city. They were younger; their average age was thirty-five. They included women, children, adolescents, families, and a growing mix of races and cultures. They lived in rural areas and in cities large and small. Most important, they were now visible.

They lived in packing crates and in doorways. They slept on sidewalks and in public parks. They displayed Will Work for Food signs while they begged coins from passersby. They trudged the streets with their possessions in shopping carts. Thus, the homeless came face-to-face with Americans who had homes and jobs.

As the visible presence of the homeless began to concern the American public, the homeless themselves began to speak out about their plight. Some spoke to Congress and to governmental committees tasked with funding programs for the homeless. Street newspapers became a new voice for the homeless. Usually published with the aid of nonhomeless people, street newspapers contain stories, poems, and essays that express the viewpoints of homeless contributors. Street newspapers publicize the frustrations of the homeless and announce to the papers' readers: Until housed people, governments, and the homeless work together to relieve the problem, homelessness will continue to be a blight upon America's social landscape.

1

A National Problem

MITCH SNYDER, A HOMELESS activist with the Community for Creative Non-Violence (CCNV), estimated in 1982 that more than 2 million Americans were homeless. Yet no official studies were undertaken until 1984, when analysts with the Department of Housing and Urban Development (HUD) estimated that the homeless population numbered between 250,000 and 350,000. In 1990 the Census Bureau attempted to include all homeless people in the national census for the first time in U.S. history. The bureau counted about 459,000 people in shelters, very cheap hotels, and in visible street locations.

The 1990 census did not end the public debate about the number of Americans who are homeless. In 1995 the National Alliance to End Homelessness estimated that 750,000 Americans are homeless on any given night and that as many as 2 million people will experience homelessness within a year. The National Coalition for the Homeless stated in 1996 that 12 million of the adult residents of the United States have been homeless at some point in their lives.

Counting the homeless

Counting the homeless accurately is impossible, yet recognizing the difference between scientific numbers and persuasive numbers is important. Scientific numbers are documented. That is, scientific numbers reflect who did the counting, what was counted, and under what circumstances the count was taken. Persuasive numbers are not

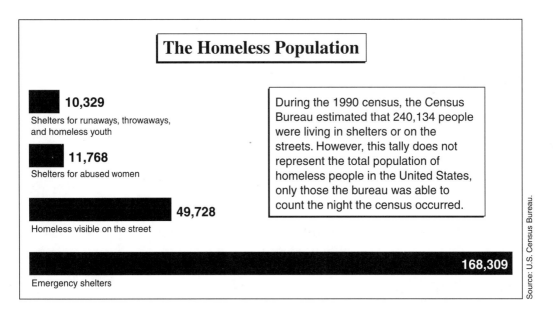

The Homeless Population

10,329
Shelters for runaways, throwaways, and homeless youth

11,768
Shelters for abused women

49,728
Homeless visible on the street

168,309
Emergency shelters

During the 1990 census, the Census Bureau estimated that 240,134 people were living in shelters or on the streets. However, this tally does not represent the total population of homeless people in the United States, only those the bureau was able to count the night the census occurred.

Source: U.S. Census Bureau.

documented. For example, when reporters questioned Mitch Snyder's high estimate of homeless people, he responded: "Everybody said we want a number. . . . We got on the phone, we made a lot of calls, we talked to a lot of people, and we said, 'Okay, here are some numbers.' They have no meaning, no value." He added that unless a problem such as homelessness is estimated in millions, the problem will not gain the media attention necessary to publicize the plight and eventually address it. Snyder was correct. His high estimates gained media attention, raised public awareness, and encouraged HUD to undertake its 1984 scientific study. Snyder and CCNV members later camped out for seven weeks near the U.S. Capitol until Congress passed its first homeless assistance act in 1987.

Although persuasive numbers may be disputed by scientific methods, scientific numbers may not always be precise either. For example, some homeless people are difficult to find. They find shelter in locations that most housed people view as dangerous or unapproachable. Therefore, census takers may not seek out the hidden homeless who live in vehicles, tents, tunnels, caves, and boxcars, places which 75 percent of formerly homeless people report having lived in at one time or another. In

1990, for instance, New York City's Metropolitan Transit Authority believed that more than 6,000 people were living in railroad tunnels around Grand Central Station and Penn Station. Yet only a few bold reporters and writers have dared to descend underground to interview these people.

Researchers and census takers may also overlook the neat and clean street homeless who do not rely on shelters. Nor will statistics include unreported children of homeless parents who fear losing custody of their children if their circumstances were known to authorities. Most researchers do not count as homeless the families who live in government subsidized housing, whereas people who live in welfare hotels while awaiting subsidized housing are counted as homeless. Furthermore, migrant workers, who typically live in a series of substandard barracks and do not have homes of their own, are not officially counted as homeless.

Persuasion or awareness?

Persuasive numbers may include the 5.3 million very-low-income families who are an accident or an illness away from becoming homeless. Scientific numbers seldom include these at-risk people among those in need of shelter. Persuasive numbers may also include an estimate of several million people living temporarily with friends or relatives, as well as people who are homeless for only a short while. Scientific numbers, such as the U.S. census, do not count "doubled-up" persons as homeless.

Activists and alarmists issue numbers as a call to awareness—a challenge to fix the problem. Agencies, institutions, and responsible advocacy groups respond with numbers that are necessary for budgeting money to fix the problem. Regardless of numbers, homelessness is unarguably a national problem that calls for solutions. According to the National Coalition for the Homeless, "More important than knowing the precise number of people who experience homelessness is our progress in ending it."

The homeless themselves call out for understanding and solutions. Said one homeless mother to a U.S. House budget committee: "What do you tell your children after you have four years of college and end up in a welfare hotel. You tell your children to go to school so they can support themselves so you don't end up in the situation—but it happened to me." Said another, "No matter what we say we can never fully communicate how we feel since none of you have lived as we have." One woman pleaded with the budget committee to visit a shelter: "Even though you are so far removed from the situation, being part of Congress, you really do need to leave those things behind and go." To understand homelessness is to see and recognize the individual faces of the homeless.

The changing face of homelessness

Of the single men who make up nearly half the homeless population, approximately one-third have served their

Single men currently make up 45 percent of the total homeless population.

country in the U.S. armed forces. More than 80 percent of homeless veterans are high school graduates. One-third have attended or graduated from college. Some suffer from mental and physical disabilities as a direct result of active duty in the military. Most are veterans of more recent wars. For example, about 40–60 percent of homeless veterans served in the armed forces during the Vietnam War. Veterans of the Persian Gulf War have also become homeless.

John Wimberly, pastor of Western Presbyterian Church in Washington, D.C., has observed the changing face of homelessness during the thirteen years that his church has operated a breakfast program for the homeless. Wimberly believes that "the homeless population is becoming younger." Twelve years ago, most participants in the breakfast program were mentally ill or had drug and alcohol problems. "Now," observes Wimberly, "a high percentage are just what I would call poor people."

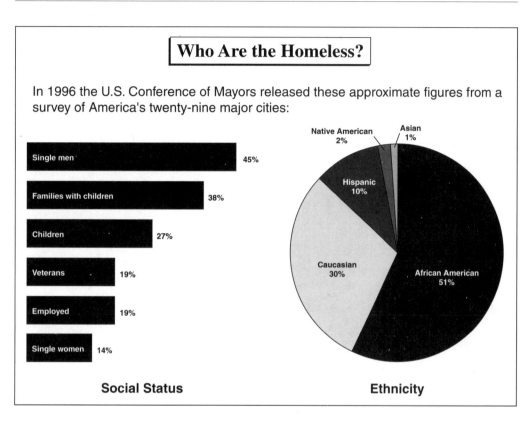

Who Are the Homeless?

In 1996 the U.S. Conference of Mayors released these approximate figures from a survey of America's twenty-nine major cities:

Social Status

- Single men: 45%
- Families with children: 38%
- Children: 27%
- Veterans: 19%
- Employed: 19%
- Single women: 14%

Ethnicity

- African American: 51%
- Caucasian: 30%
- Hispanic: 10%
- Native American: 2%
- Asian: 1%

According to Wimberly, the poor are often

a married couple living in public housing. They get divorced, which means that everybody in the family ends up homeless. They were able to scrape by on two marginal incomes, but they find out they can't make ends meet when they're by themselves. In some ways, I think the changing nature of the homeless population is more significant than the numbers.

The changing image of the homeless is observed nationwide. Many of today's homeless are people who have worked all their lives. When they lose their jobs, they lose their homes. Unless they have considerable savings, or the support of family and friends, they end up on a waiting list for subsidized housing and must turn to government and charities for food and shelter. In 1995, requests for shelter by homeless families in America's major cities increased by 15 percent over the previous year. A fourth of these requests went unmet, due in part to family-shelter space limitations during times of immediate need.

Nearly one-third of all homeless men have served in the U.S. armed forces, and many are war veterans. Here, a homeless veteran and his companion sit inside a camp set up to help homeless veterans in Boston.

In Massachusetts in 1988, 75 percent of all homeless people were children and their parents. In Atlanta in 1993, families with children made up 57 percent of the people who requested shelter from Atlanta's Task Force hot line. Of those families, 86 percent were single-parent families. Although 18 percent of families who requested shelter had a family member who was employed, their wages did not cover the costs of housing, food, child care, and health expenses for the family.

Homelessness is not confined to cities, nor do all the nation's homeless live in shelters or on the street. A 1996 study by the U.S. Department of Agriculture revealed that homeless people in small towns and rural areas are most likely to be white, female, married, employed, and homeless for the first time. Because fewer shelters are available in rural areas, the rural homeless are more likely to live in a car or a camper, or with relatives.

Poverty

Whether urban or rural, homelessness is not a crisis unto itself. Homelessness is rooted in extreme poverty.

According to the Interagency Council on the Homeless, a homeless person has an average income of less than $150 per month, or less than $1,800 per year. In 1996 an individual needed $8,000 a year to live above the threshold of poverty.

In 1995 more than 37 million Americans lived below the poverty level. Of these, 40 percent were children and about 11 percent were families. Yet, among black and Hispanic families with children, more than one-third continue to live in poverty. With the nation's child poverty rate at 21 percent overall, it is no coincidence that families with children are among the fastest growing segments of the homeless population.

Homelessness looms when a family's income is insufficient to cover basic living expenses. Federal programs such as Aid to Families with Dependent Children (AFDC) cannot meet the financial needs of poor families. In 1995, AFDC families received about $135 per person per month. Only 20 percent of all AFDC families received a housing subsidy—government aid to pay a portion of their rent.

Homelessness also threatens when a family member gets sick. Between 1987 and 1992, household health care costs rose 56 percent. For people without health insurance or work-related health benefits, a serious illness or an accident may dictate the choice between paying the medical bills or paying the rent.

Homelessness becomes a reality when relatives or friends cannot help because they themselves are poor; because they themselves live in crowded or substandard housing; because they themselves lose welfare benefits due to government budget cuts.

Public awareness grows

After advocates began to speak out for the homeless in the 1980s, the news media focused more attention on the issue. Newspapers printed photographs of the homeless sleeping on outdoor heating grates. Television newscasters reported children living in squalid, unheated apartments and boarded-up buildings. Awareness and concern mounted as people saw the changing face of homelessness: more young people, more women, more ethnic minorities, more people scavenging in dumpsters in suburban parking lots.

Although the media devoted more coverage to the crisis during holidays and winter months, the public perceived that homelessness was not a seasonal problem. Nor was it a problem that would solve itself. Furthermore, as activists proclaimed that the homeless population was rising into the millions, the media and the public perceived that homelessness was not only a crisis but an embarrassment within a nation of freedom and wealth.

Government helps the homeless

Advocates and citizens turned to the federal government to aid the homeless. Congress responded by approving the 1987 Stewart B. McKinney Homeless Assistance Act. This important statute approved $443 million in homeless aid for 1987 and $616 million for 1988, and it established the Interagency Council on the Homeless. The McKinney Act funded programs for emergency food and shelter, medical and mental-health care, education and job training opportunities, and permanent housing for applicants who qualified for housing assistance.

Congress extended the McKinney Act in 1993 by authorizing $150 million to construct single-room occupancy housing (SROs) for the homeless. During 1995 and 1996, however, the executive and legislative branches of the federal government disagreed on budget issues, and the debates continue to affect AFDC and the McKinney Act. In August 1996, President Bill Clinton approved and signed the Personal Responsibility and Work Opportunity Reconciliation Act of 1996, commonly referred to as "welfare reform." The purpose of welfare reform is to move people off of welfare and into employment. The welfare reform bill cut $54 billion over six years from federally funded programs that serve as a safety net for impoverished families.

In essence, federal programs such as AFDC were handed over to the individual states, along with block grants to create programs that would replace AFDC and emergency assistance units. New block-grant funding for states took effect July 1, 1997. Within a year after President Clinton signed the welfare reform bill, *Newsweek* reported the number of women and children on welfare dropped by nearly 2 million. However, phrases such as "welfare reform" and "the unbalanced budget" continue to identify ongoing conflicts among policy makers whose votes create and fund programs that serve the impoverished and the homeless.

Demonstrators outside the White House protest the Personal Responsibility and Work Opportunity Reconciliation Act of 1996, commonly known as welfare reform.

Effects of federal budget cuts

Those who favor budget cuts want private charities to offer more financial aid to the homeless. Homeless advocates and those who already aid the homeless claim that private charities, as well as corporations and foundations, already provide all the help they can.

One of the country's largest agencies working for the homeless is the Partnership for the Homeless in New York City. The Partnership for the Homeless oversees shelter space in 150 churches and synagogues, reimbursing them for food and fuel expenses. Facing 25 percent in federal and state budget cuts in 1996, the partnership's president, Joel Sesser, stated that "charitable donations can't make up for such a large loss." He also worries about government cuts to welfare: "If these people lose their benefits, not all of them will find or succeed at jobs—they have so many serious problems. A lot will then be pushed into homelessness." Officials in twenty-nine cities describe the result of proposed federal budget cuts in welfare, Medicaid, and housing assistance as "a bleak picture" that will lead to increased homelessness and fewer housing options.

Newsweek reported in August 1997 that homelessness and visits to food banks have risen in areas that have the toughest new welfare laws. Florida and Wisconsin, for example, dropped their welfare recipients as soon as welfare

Police officers confront a homeless man who had been sleeping on the steps of a New York City post office branch. Many cities enforce trespass laws that prohibit homeless people from camping in public places.

reform allowed. On the other hand, about a fourth of America's fastest-growing small companies have hired welfare recipients, and 60 percent of these employers say they are willing to hire them. But a big question remains: Do the majority of welfare recipients have the life skills necessary to hold a job? Or will loss of benefits plunge them into homelessness and increased poverty?

As welfare reform and budget battles continue, the public and the media continue to ask who will help the homeless, the most destitute, the people who for one reason or another cannot make ends meet. Jonathan Alter says in *Newsweek,* "Yes, the hardcore welfare recipients shall always be with us, beset by personal demons." Sister Connie Driscoll, president of Chicago's St. Martin de Porres House of Hope, says, "We've got to remember, really deep down in our hearts, that all the homeless people out there are our brothers and our sisters. Their children are our children. We have got to find a way for them to survive in a better life. That's the bottom line." However, many jurisdictions prefer to eliminate the poor and the homeless by forcing them out of sight or out of town.

"Not in my backyard"

While preparing for the 1996 Summer Olympics, officials in Atlanta enforced several city ordinances designed to keep homeless people out of sight. One ordinance banned people from remaining in parking lots. A 1996 ordinance in Austin, Texas, prohibits camping on public property. In Seattle, trespass laws make it illegal to rest on benches in downtown public areas.

Of the fifty largest cities in the United States, five are named by the National Law Center on Homelessness and Poverty as having the "meanest streets" because of regulations that prohibit homeless residents from using public spaces. The five—Atlanta, San Francisco, New York, Dallas, and San Diego—have cracked down on the homeless in response to citizens and business owners who want the homeless off the streets. More than half of America's largest cities have engaged in police "sweeps" of homeless people. By 1995 San Francisco had swept its streets by issuing over 27,000 arrests and citations. Homeless advocates claim that these cities are "criminalizing" the homeless.

Bishop John E. McCarthy of Austin points out that the homeless must congregate downtown because that is where they can find food and day-labor jobs, jobs in which they are paid daily for their work. He said in *National Catholic Reporter,* "We encourage them to work, yet we want them, without transportation, to get out of the city. How do they get back? Until either the community or the churches of the community work together to provide a real solution, I think, the present ban on camping is cruel."

Maria Foscarinis, executive director of the National Law Center, said in 1996 that

> a majority of Americans are sympathetic to homeless people and would like to see an increase in aid for them. But this desire isn't being translated into supportive action by politicians, who instead try to find a quick fix through the ordinances, zoning laws and building codes. They want homeless people out, but there's nowhere for them to go.

The National Law Center learned that twenty-one projects to assist the homeless were halted, six facilities were forced to close, and two were relocated—all because of

opposition from people who want the homeless housed somewhere, elsewhere, but "not in my backyard." This "not in my backyard" viewpoint—the NIMBY view—is voiced by neighborhood residents who fear a decline in their property value if the poor or homeless are sheltered nearby. The NIMBY view reflects fear of drug dealers and users associated with the homeless. It reflects concern for family and neighborhood safety. It voices what some advocates call "compassion fatigue."

John Steinbruck, senior pastor of Luther Place Memorial Church in Washington, D.C., said in 1995, "When new people move in and decide that our work with the homeless conflicts with their vision of the area, then they will do what they can to terminate our programs." Luther Place offers food, shelter, and counseling in several buildings on its campus. Steinbruck believes that his block is "probably the most drug-free block in Washington. We know who's doing what on the street, and we will give [drug dealers] no peace if they're in our territory." Even so, the church's homeless program has spent hundreds of thousands of dollars in court costs in recent years fighting the NIMBY outlook.

Withdrawing and adding services

Some cities seek to drive away the homeless by withdrawing services. For example, Roseville, California, refused to open its armory as a shelter during the winter of 1994–1995, even though local churches promised to pay the costs. Roseville officials dismantled encampments, threw away property, and issued citations to homeless people living in public places.

The National Law Center responds to such decisions by saying, "In the absence of sufficient shelter space, homeless people literally have nowhere else to go—or be—than the streets and other public places. Cities that punish their homeless residents for these activities essentially punish them for being homeless."

On the other hand, several cities have responded to NIMBYism by passing laws that help the homeless. Dade County, Florida's 1 percent tax on meals purchased at restaurants provides more than $400,000 a year toward facilities and services for the homeless. Miami provides homeless people with safe zones in which they cannot be arrested. In West Hollywood, California, service providers—rather than police officers—make the first contact with homeless persons. Seattle officials offered funds for downtown public toilets, showers, and laundry facilities available free of charge for homeless people.

Civil rights for the homeless

For every victory scored by advocates and volunteers who work with the homeless, new opposition arises. Of America's fifty cities that carried out street sweeps of homeless people in 1996, nearly 80 percent were enforcing laws that prohibit or restrict begging. Advocates suggest that such ordinances violate the civil rights of homeless people.

In 1992, U.S. district judge Robert W. Sweet ruled against a New York City antibegging statute, saying that the statute was unconstitutional under the First Amendment to the U.S. Constitution. In 1994 Judge Frederic N. Smalkin ruled against a similar ordinance in Baltimore. The *Baltimore Sun* responded by writing that panhandlers—street beggars—are "looking for the next hit of crack or scrounging up the price of some cheap booze. The crack or the booze may be the reason the panhandler is on the street asking for handouts in the first place. Giving money only subsidizes the panhandlers' habits."

Some people blame the poor and the homeless for engaging in habits or lifestyles that lead to their predicament. Others blame government and society for creating or allowing circumstances that thrust their fellow citizens into homelessness and poverty. Studies continue to address the question of what causes homelessness.

2

Causes of Homelessness

SOCIOLOGIST CHRISTOPHER JENCKS wrote in 1994, "If you have no salable skills, no claim to government benefits, no friends or relatives willing to help out, and if you spend whatever money you have on crack [cocaine], you are likely to become homeless. If no one drank, took drugs, lost contact with reality, or messed up at work, homelessness would be rare. It is the combination of personal vulnerability and political indifference that has left people in the streets."

Whether politicians are indifferent to the homeless continues to be a matter of opinion. The National Coalition for the Homeless (NCH) is a leading advocacy group that confronts the political reasons why people may become or remain homeless. NCH supports its position with documented surveys, scholastic studies, and traceable figures. According to NCH, the fact that some people are more vulnerable to homelessness—that is, more likely than others to become homeless—is most often a result of two recent trends: rising poverty and a shortage of affordable housing.

Poverty

The inability of poor people to afford housing is certainly the leading cause of homelessness, and the most simple explanation of the national crisis. However, the reason why some people are poor while others are not, and the

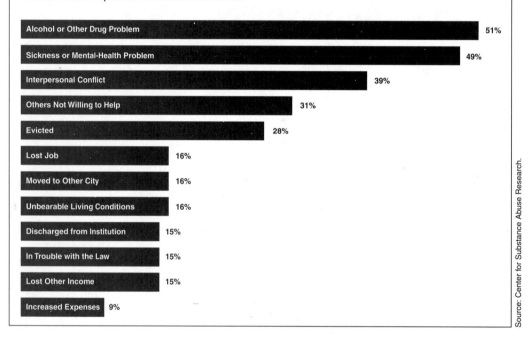

Reasons for Homelessness

A 1996 survey by researchers at Mental Health Services West—a community mental-health agency in Portland, Oregon—revealed the reasons for their clients' most recent episode of homelessness:

Alcohol or Other Drug Problem	51%
Sickness or Mental-Health Problem	49%
Interpersonal Conflict	39%
Others Not Willing to Help	31%
Evicted	28%
Lost Job	16%
Moved to Other City	16%
Unbearable Living Conditions	16%
Discharged from Institution	15%
In Trouble with the Law	15%
Lost Other Income	15%
Increased Expenses	9%

Source: Center for Substance Abuse Research.

reason why some people become homeless or remain homeless while others do not, is far more complex. The reason why *one* person is homeless is as unique as that individual's life story.

During congressional hearings on the rising problem of homelessness in the 1980s, E. Marrero said, "I want to state that my becoming homeless is not representative of all homeless people. . . . My story is unique in and of itself, just as there are stories among you of success and failure, triumph and tragedy; unique because they are ours, yours and mine."

J. Wilkins testified, "I am homeless because of family problems. I have cerebral palsy." L. Stanley, an adolescent, said, "Living in the hotel for a while and I started like hanging out with other kids and they were like stealing and I didn't want to do it, so when I hang out with them I got bad and my mother sent me away to a group home for a while. And it was bad there too." Others explained why they were caught up in the cycle of homelessness. As D. Navarez explained, "I can become homeless again if I cannot afford to pay my rent or my children can't live or survive, so it's all the same thing. . . . It's like a vicious cycle."

The common bond among these unique individuals is poverty. Being poor means making choices about how to spend a limited amount of money. Housing, food, child care, health care, clothing, and education are choices. Chemical dependency on alcohol or drugs may be a choice for an addicted person who has not sought help. Mental illness, although not a choice, may impair a person's ability to make healthy choices or to hold a job. Faced with choosing between housing, which absorbs a high proportion of income, and all other needs combined, poor people may choose the shelter or the street.

Working and living in poverty

The opportunity to work for a living wage is not available to all people. A scarcity of jobs is not the problem. The challenge for low-skilled and low-educated workers is to find a job that enables them to pay their living expenses. According to the Bureau of Labor Statistics, nearly 70 percent of new jobs created between 1988 and 2000 are, or will be, in services and retail trade. These jobs rarely pay more than minimum wage. A 1996 HUD study showed that in forty-five states and the District of Columbia, families would need to earn at least double the minimum wage to afford a two-bedroom unit priced at fair market rent (FMR).

FMRs are determined by HUD to be the monthly amounts needed to rent privately owned safe, sanitary, nonluxury housing with appropriate facilities such as a kitchen and a bathroom. In all fifty states, a full-time employee earning the minimum wage cannot afford a one-bedroom FMR unit. This may help explain why one in five homeless persons in America's twenty-nine largest cities works either full-time or part-time and is still a victim of poverty.

In addition to eroding opportunities for living-wage work, changes in government benefits contribute to rising poverty. Even before its repeal in August 1996, the AFDC program was not sufficient to meet the needs of poor families with children. In all states except Alaska, AFDC benefits did not equal the rent on a two-bedroom rental unit for a family of three. In 1996 the purchase power—the value of purchases—of AFDC and food stamps combined was below the poverty level in all fifty states.

Single people also are affected by changes in government benefits. General assistance has been reduced or eliminated in several states. According to HUD housing recommendations, Supplemental Security Income (SSI) benefits in every state would have to be more than doubled in order to provide adequate housing for SSI recipients.

Unfortunately, not all homeless people qualified for benefits in the past. A 1987 Urban Institute interview of homeless singles in soup kitchens, shelters, and gathering places showed that 97 percent were too young to receive old-age benefits and the 80 percent of singles without children had monthly cash incomes below $250.

A doctor working in a mobile clinic examines a homeless infant. Without health care insurance, homeless people often have to forgo medical care.

Affordable health care

A lack of affordable health care can plunge people with low incomes into homelessness. America has no government-regulated health care system. Unless people receive health care or medical insurance as an employment benefit, they must purchase it themselves. Health insurance can cost as much per month as low-income rent. Therefore, it is not surprising that in 1995 about 39 million Americans had no health care insurance.

Government benefits such as worker's compensation, Social Security Disability, and state disability help sick or disabled people, but often this income does not sufficiently meet the needs of a family. The Sjoblom family in Matawan, New Jersey, lost their home as a result of Russell Sjoblom's disabling work-related injury. Although his wife, Diane, worked to support them and their two school-age children, additional compensation and government aid could not cover their medical and household expenses. Regulations and long waits blocked their move to public housing. They were evicted from their own home and were thrust into homelessness in September 1995. NCH publicized their dilemma as typical of working families who become homeless when sickness or injury strikes.

Mental illness

Mental illness can also lead to homelessness. Christopher Jencks reports that in 1987 at least 1.7 million people had mental problems so severe they could not hold a job; of those, 100,000 were homeless. NCH reported in 1996 that about one-third of the single adult homeless population suffers from mental illness, yet less than one-fourth have ever been in a mental hospital.

In 1965 Congress established Medicaid to pay health care bills for poor patients. However, health care for mentally ill people changed after Medicaid was established, and changed again in 1972 when SSI was established. Medicaid and SSI did not cover anyone in a state mental hospital. As mental hospitals faced rising costs, they reduced the number of beds available and discharged patients to the care of Medicaid and SSI. As a result of the Community Health Centers Act of 1963, about 430,000 mentally ill people were discharged. Only those patients diagnosed as dangerous to themselves or to others remained hospitalized.

If discharged patients had the support of friends or family, or if they were able to apply for and receive approxi-

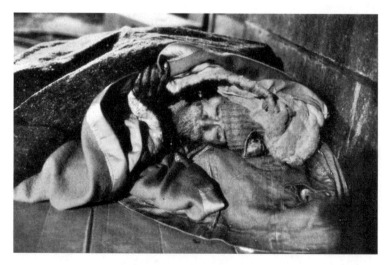

An elderly man huddles under blankets as he sleeps on the ground. Many homeless people suffer from mental illnesses that prevent them from functioning in society.

mately $500 in monthly benefits, they were able to survive outside a mental hospital. However, one leading characteristic of mental illness is the lack of ability to maintain healthy relationships. Sociologist Peter Rossi's street surveys of homeless people revealed that about half of those questioned say they have no good friends. More than a third report having no friends at all. Thus, many of the patients who did not possess the support of friends or family ended up on the streets. As for these, limited employment skills and characteristics of their illness kept many from earning a living.

According to NCH, at least half of the mentally ill homeless also have alcohol or drug problems. Their combined problems of mental illness and chemical dependency are further compounded by the chaos of life on the street.

Chemical dependency

Chemical dependency is another social problem that can lead to homelessness. Although no one can explain precisely why, America has always had high levels of alcohol abuse. However, alcoholism alone does not cause homelessness. In the early 1980s, the one-third of the homeless population with severe alcohol problems was about the same percentage as in previous generations. Then around 1984 a significant event reshaped the American drug scene, and had a profound effect on homelessness. That event was the arrival of crack cocaine. Cheaper than alcohol, crack could be purchased for $10 wherever the homeless congregated. Homelessness spread in the late 1980s as criminals made crack available in smaller doses at lower costs. Today a $3 dose of crack must be compared to the $8 cost of a bed in a New York or Chicago cubicle hotel. When faced with a choice between a dose of crack or a bed for the night, chemically addicted people may favor their addiction over shelter. For this reason, Christopher Jencks calls crack cocaine the only new factor affecting homelessness since 1984.

Crack lures the rich and the poor into crippling addiction. The NBA's first-round draft choice in 1981 was an Indiana basketball player who enjoyed a six-year professional career. In 1993 he entered South Bend, Indiana's Center for the Homeless. He did not go there to mentor the homeless, but because he himself was destitute. The primary cause of his homelessness: cocaine addiction.

Alcohol abuse and the lure of inexpensive crack cocaine can lead to homelessness either through use or through removal of government benefits for users. Federal legislation enacted in 1996 denies SSI benefits, Social Security Disability Insurance, and Medicaid access to people whose addictions are considered to be a contributing factor to their disability. As of 1997 these regulations will affect as many as 50,000 people per year. And although treatment programs are available, 80 percent of programs surveyed in 1992 could not meet rising demands. Homeless clients had to be turned away.

Chemical dependency sometimes leads to violence. A 1994 study of ten homeless families in Georgia found that three of the mothers were drug addicts, two wanted to get their children away from fathers who were using drugs, and two were escaping abuse in which drugs were involved. One of the mothers said of a family member, "He's so thoroughly on drugs until it's awful. I have let him be my downfall a lot."

Domestic violence

Domestic violence has been identified as one of the major causes of homelessness. A 1990 Ford Foundation study found that 50 percent of homeless women and children were fleeing abuse. About half the nation's twenty-nine major cities name domestic violence as a primary cause of homelessness.

When a woman leaves an abusive relationship, she often has nowhere to go. If she does not have the support of family or friends, she may enter a shelter for abused women, where her stay will be limited to the length of time allowed by the shelter. In rural areas, women who flee domestic violence may not find shelter. Or battered women's shelters may be filled to capacity. For example, the Virginia Coalition for the Homeless reported in 1995 that 35 percent of Virginia's sheltered homeless are victims of family violence. However, more than 2,000 women seeking shelter from domestic abuse were turned away because of lack of space.

While seeking shelter, or while in a shelter, a woman without resources must also seek employment. A minimally educated woman with limited skills is handicapped in her search for a job that pays a living wage. Lack of adequate shelter and long waiting lists for housing subsidies mean that battered women are often forced to choose between abusive relationships and homelessness.

Children and adolescents who are abused at home, in foster homes, or in the homes of other family members and friends may escape the violence by entering a shelter. However, if shelter space is not available, abused young people must choose between danger at home and danger on the street.

Crumbling family structure

While homelessness became a national issue during the 1980s, changes were also taking place within families. Between 1969 and 1989, the number of extremely low-income single women with children doubled. Until 1979 half of these mothers lived with at least one other adult. By 1989 only 36 percent did. If single mothers lose their job, their benefits, or the financial support of friends or family, they are at high risk for homelessness.

Of homeless mothers, 65 percent did not complete high school, and they became mothers at a younger age than did girls who finished school. Homes for the Homeless in New York City reported in 1996 that homeless mothers are the poorest and fastest growing segment of the welfare population and that daughters of teenage mothers are more likely to become teenage mothers themselves. More than 500,000

Homeless and the mother of six, this recovering addict is just one of the many homeless people who suffer from chemical dependency.

teenage girls give birth each year. Many are repeating the family cycle of early parenthood, welfare, and shelters or the street.

The number of children in foster care has increased by 64 percent since 1986. During the same period, homelessness among young, single, female-headed households increased fivefold. One in five homeless mothers already has children in foster care, while more than a third of homeless mothers are under investigation for child abuse or neglect.

Welfare reform

Although homeless mothers are the fastest growing segment of the welfare population, welfare benefits have diminished since 1996. Welfare reform, officially titled the Personal Responsibility and Work Opportunity Reconciliation Act of 1996, was designed to encourage those who receive government benefits to substitute work for welfare. Qualifications for benefits separated people who were deemed able to work from those deemed disabled, and they placed limits on how long unemployed people can receive welfare benefits.

Welfare reform has challenged the poor, the undereducated, and those who try to help them find work. Janet

Schrader, a welfare caseworker in Alexandria, Virginia, wrote in the *Washington Post* in May 1997,

> Imagine my calling an employer and saying: "I have a woman around [age] 40 with no diploma or GED, with limited work experience in fast food or housekeeping, who really wants to work but who has had some problems with alcohol abuse in the past and whose teenage sons are getting into trouble, causing her to be called to school or court, which might affect her ability to get to work or to get to work on time. But other than that she's good to go." And I would love for that employer to say, "Send her right over." Such a scenario would happen only in my dreams.

Schrader described one woman entering the new welfare program:

> She started working for a department store full-time, $6.50 an hour, in June 1996 and was off welfare by July. A few weeks ago, she called to tell me that her hours are being reduced and if she loses any more time, she may not be able to pay the rent. . . . When President Clinton signed the new national welfare legislation in late August [1996], some lawmakers and many advocates for the poor decried the law. They painted a bleak picture of families living on the streets and children going without food. At the time, I thought they were overreacting. Now I'm beginning to think that maybe the alarmists were right.

If former welfare recipients are to succeed at work, they will most likely need state-supplied child care and transportation, as well as employers who understand their lack of basic work skills. Missouri and Illinois now guarantee child care and transportation assistance to former welfare recipients who land jobs. Allocations for child care go directly to the child-care center, rather than as welfare to the parents.

Some employers offer a buddy system to help ease people into a job. One corporate executive was quoted in *Newsweek:* "The first thing you learn is they come in late. They've often never owned an alarm clock. If you work with them, give them a 'buddy' at the start, they often turn into outstanding employees." Another executive said that people must learn technical skills and how to behave in a job. His company's ads for low-wage work went unanswered. As a result he turned to "job intermediaries" who help train and place people in jobs they can handle. Without such intercession for welfare recipients, housed and unhoused, welfare reform alone may not improve the economy or reduce homelessness and poverty.

Inadequate low-rent housing

Coupled with rising poverty, the other major trend that leads to homelessness is the combination of the shortage of adequate affordable housing and the inadequacy of housing assistance programs. This trend has affected single people and families in a number of ways.

Rooms without kitchens, rooms without bathrooms, and windowless cubicles in "cage" hotels—all designed for single room occupancy (SRO)—diminished steadily in the 1960s and 1970s. The 1980 census counted only 28,000 people living in rooms costing less than $4 per night. The 1990 census did not include housing of this type in its criteria.

Monthly rent of a reasonably clean and safe SRO in 1960 equaled twelve to twenty hours of minimum-wage work per month. Monthly rent of an SRO in 1995 equaled forty hours of minimum-wage work per month to live in squalid quarters in deteriorating neighborhoods. However, the federal government sets subsidized rents at 30 percent of a tenant's income. Therefore, an SRO tenant would need an income of $500 per month in 1995 to afford a room costing $150. Less than 5 percent of homeless single adults have incomes that high.

Families in need of adequate housing face several challenges. Between 1973 and 1993, 2.2 million low-rent units disappeared from the market, while the number of low-income renters rose from 7.4 million to 11.2 million. According to NCH, the resulting shortage of 4.7 million affordable housing units is the largest shortage on record.

Of the low-rent units available before 1993, many had no central heat or hot water, no complete kitchens or bathrooms. Families who could afford not to live in these conditions moved to safer, cleaner neighborhoods where rent was higher. Although vacancy rates rose as people moved out, the vacancies were for undesirable, unsafe housing in neighborhoods that eventually gave way to the bulldozer and the wrecker's ball.

For the adequate housing that remained, affordability became the central issue. Today's low-income renters pay more for housing than they did a decade or two ago. A 1996 HUD study learned that almost 95 percent of renters with "worst case needs" paid over half of their income for housing. Worst-case needs include renters with incomes below 50 percent of their area median income who pay more than half their income for rent and utilities, or who live in substandard housing. Of the 5.3 million unassisted households determined by HUD as having worst-case needs, the largest increase occurred among families with children, the elderly, and the very-low-income disabled.

Inadequate housing assistance

Availability and affordability are linked to another challenge: inadequate housing assistance programs. Housing assistance refers primarily to low-income housing units or housing programs that are funded by the federal government. Section 8 housing, named for the 1974 legislation that created it, involves the use of subsidies—assistance based on a tenant's ability to pay. Subsidies are awarded in the form of certificates or as vouchers.

Section 8 certificates are awarded to public housing authorities (PHAs), who in turn distribute them to qualified tenants. Tenants must then find housing that meets government standards and landlords who agree to accept Section 8 certificates. A tenant's subsidy provides the landlord with the difference between 30 percent of the tenant's income and the community FMR. If a tenant moves, he or she takes the certificate to another landlord at another approved unit.

Section 8 vouchers differ from certificates in that vouchers can be used by a tenant to pay the entire rent, if the rent does not exceed 30 percent of his or her income. However, if a unit rents for more than the standard FMR, the tenant must pay 30 percent of his or her income plus the additional amount that exceeds the FMR. Under this plan, tenants may have to pay more than 30 percent of their income for housing, even with the use of a Section 8 voucher.

Unfortunately, these housing assistance programs do not relieve the needs of the majority of at-risk people. Assistance programs also do not ease the concerns and fears of those whose only choice is a federally funded housing project designed for Section 8 tenants. One homeless woman, Susan, says, "It's impossible to pay rent, like two hundred and something dollars, and then all there is is the projects. And most people, like me, I would have hated to move in the projects with Terry [her daughter]." Rather than risk the projects, Susan moved to a shelter.

Delays and limitations

Although 40 percent of all impoverished families are eligible for housing assistance, only 26 percent of eligible households receive it. Even for those who seek it, relief is not immediate. Applicants who apply for public housing in America's twenty-nine major cities must wait an average of seventeen months for assistance. Applicants for housing vouchers wait an average of thirty-nine months. Section 8 housing applicants wait an average of forty months; some wait for as long as six years. They may wait while sick or disabled, or in the homes of friends or relatives, in high-crime neighborhoods, in unsanitary or unsafe housing, or in a series of shelters. Therefore those who wait in shelters sleep in beds that will not be available to other homeless people needing shelter.

Most Section 8 contracts with the federal government expire after fifteen or twenty years. Therefore, contracts made in the 1970s that provide certificates and vouchers for nearly 1 million families are expiring in the 1990s. In addition, building owners who signed Section 8 contracts after 1980 are allowed to withdraw from their contracts at five-year intervals. Although HUD has not kept records of owners who withdraw early, records do show that no new vouchers or certificates were awarded for Section 8 housing in 1995. Furthermore, the federal budget has not allocated enough money to renew all the Section 8 contracts that HUD and some building owners want to renew. If Section 8 housing is severely reduced or eliminated, it will result in the loss of tens of thousands of affordable housing units.

Accountability

Service providers claim that personal responsibility is an issue when addressing the causes of homelessness and poverty. That is, if people make choices that undermine their ability to earn a living, pay their own way, and maintain healthy relationships, they may be putting themselves at risk of becoming homeless. If people with a limited income spend money that should go toward paying the rent on nonessential items, they risk being evicted for nonpayment of rent. Chicago's Sister Connie Driscoll says,

> Many people have been evicted from their apartments not because they *couldn't* pay their rent, but because they *didn't* pay it. Some spent the rent money on drugs, of course, while others used it to buy big-ticket items. . . . After a while, you find yourself saying, "Wait a minute. Housing isn't the issue here. The issue is personal responsibility and accountability. You've got to get your life together. We can't do this for you, we can only give you the tools. You've got to do it."

Determining the causes of homelessness has not reduced the number of people who are homeless. Not all homeless people turn to shelters. A unique way of life exists for the homeless who live outside the shelter system or the welfare system. These people are sometimes labeled as vagrants, panhandlers, bag ladies, and bums. They live on the streets.

3

Life on the Streets

In JANUARY 1996, New York City Coalition for the Homeless director Mary Brosnahan said, "We don't even try to estimate the number of people" sleeping on the street. Although 86,000 people used New York City's shelter system in 1995, this number could not account for people who choose the street over shelters. Rather than count heads, Brosnahan's agency tries to attract street people whom she describes as "at the end of the line."

At the end of the line

People described as being at the end of the line seldom rely on traditional resources such as shelters, government agencies, and housing programs designed to aid the poor. They are the men and women who decline rides to shelters on bitter nights but may accept a blanket or a cup of coffee from concerned citizens.

Housed people have been heard to say that some homeless people purposely choose their way of life. President Ronald Reagan said in 1984, "One problem we've had is the people who are sleeping on grates—the homeless who are homeless, you might say, by choice." During an interview with authors David A. Snow and Leon Anderson, an Austin police officer said street people in that city "have chosen their lifestyle" and are "content to be the way they are." However, only 2.7 percent of street people interviewed by Snow and Anderson named personal choice—independence and the adventure of the road—as their reason for being homeless. Most named unemployment, disabilities, family problems, and accidents or bad luck. That is to say, the majority viewed street life as a situation beyond their control.

The homeless who do prefer the outdoors confound those who offer them shelter. Wendy Moore, director of Roanoke Area Ministries, told the Associated Press that many transients had the flu during the winter of 1997, thereby making them more susceptible to life-threatening illnesses such as pneumonia. "Still," she said, "some people just refuse to go to shelters." The street homeless—those who refuse to sleep in shelters or who rarely sleep in one—are the portion of the homeless population that can be described as living within a separate and distinct subculture of homelessness.

The subculture of the street

Snow and Anderson conducted their field study of Austin's street people in the mid-1980s. For more than a year and a half, they interviewed and observed what they called a cross-section of Americans who happened to be homeless and living in Austin. The authors returned to

A homeless man sleeps on a steam grate in downtown Cleveland. Some homeless people opt to live on the streets rather than in shelters.

their field of study in 1990 to discover that, although the faces of the homeless had changed, and some of the service providers had changed, the day-to-day activities of Austin's street homeless were much the same as in 1984 and 1985.

Jennifer Wolch and Michael Dear studied the subculture of Skid Row in Los Angeles. Margaret Morton, a photographer and associate professor of art at the Cooper Union in New York City, descended underground to interview and photograph a subculture living in a two-and-a-half-mile-long tunnel long-abandoned by the New York Central and Hudson River Railroads. Morton calls her subjects, and others like them, the "hidden homeless." "They're not part of the homeless community," she says. "They're a kind of underground population who've been pushed out of view."

In whatever city the street homeless happen to be, their subculture reflects certain recurring characteristics, which Snow and Anderson listed in their study: mobility, self-identity, substance use, the amount of time (months or years) spent on the streets, daily routines, work or resourcefulness, and hopes for the future. Although some or all of these characteristics define the lifestyle of every homeless person, the lifestyle itself is most likely to be one of adaptation rather than choice.

When first thrust into homelessness, a person learns how to survive among others who share the same fate. How one person survives defines his or her lifestyle. When a number of people adopt similar survival methods, the result is a subculture that researchers such as Snow and Anderson can study and describe. However, as the homeless are quick to point out, each person's reasons for living within the subculture are as unique as that person's fingerprints.

Mobility

Street people are transient. Because they are nearly always on the move, their daily lives are marked by instability and change. Their mobility may mean walking the streets within one city, or it may extend from coast to coast. For example, more than half of Austin's street home-

A woman reads a magazine while standing beside shopping carts filled with her belongings. Street people are usually transient and will even move to other cities or states as the climate changes.

less came from states other than Texas. About 40 percent said they were from other Texas towns; less than 10 percent claimed Austin as home. Even so, 87 percent of all people interviewed in Austin said they had been there for less than a month. Shotgun, a homeless man who spent ten winters in Austin, told Snow and Anderson that he "tramped" his way across the country, and he proudly called himself a tramp.

Transience varies from region to region. More than half of Birmingham's street homeless claim that city as home. In Phoenix, only 7 percent say they are local residents. However, Peter Rossi's surveys of Chicago's street homeless revealed that nearly three-fourths had lived there for ten years or more. Studies by Snow and Anderson show that the majority of homeless people in northeastern cities are less likely to move than those in the south, southwest, and far west, where transients frequently move from one temperate climate to another.

When street people explain their reasons for moving from one locale to another, most say they are looking for work, for new opportunity, and that they are certain their luck will be better somewhere else. Tony, Sonny, and Ron shared their experiences with Snow and Anderson.

Tony traveled from Chicago to Baton Rouge to Houston to Austin looking for work. After he landed a job as an appliance repairman, Tony lived at the Salvation Army until he could afford an apartment. After a brief stay in a rooming house, he hit the road again. Sonny, nineteen, hitchhiked from Missouri to Tulsa, then hitched with a trucker to Austin, where he worked as a roofer's helper. After his employer refused to pay him, he moved into the backseat of a homeless coworker's car. Ron, twenty-two, moved from California to Denver to Austin as he roamed the streets of cities throughout the west. After four months in Austin, Ron left for either San Diego or Orlando. As to which temperate city he planned to go, or whether he would head west to San Diego or east to Orlando, he had not decided. But he was on the move, with the belief that life would be better down the road.

A homeless twenty-two-year-old man cries as he begs for money on the streets of San Francisco.

Many homeless people say they spend their daytime hours walking and changing street locations to avoid rob-

bery or assault by other street people, or harassment by the police. Some street people also report leaving a neighborhood to get away from street gangs or a drug culture that they want no part of. In these instances, mobility serves as a means of self-protection. Others spend their days moving from soup kitchens to the day-labor center or the welfare office, or to public washroom facilities or to a favorite spot for panhandling and sleeping. People who have entered a substance-abuse program must attend counseling sessions and 12-step meetings wherever those meetings are held. And medical care may involve another long walk.

Banjo gave Snow and Anderson another reason for mobility:

> You want to know why we're always on the move? I'll tell you why. The Sally [Salvation Army] won't let you stay but three nights for free in most places. After that you have to pay or you gotta leave. So you go to the next town, and it's the same thing. Three days and then you gotta pay or go. Now, how're you supposed to get a job and a paycheck in a new town in three days? See, that's what happens, and then they call us "transients." What're we supposed to do?

Self-identity

Homeless people report that an added burden to being homeless is the way in which society looks down on them. Street people tell of being avoided, pointed out, and laughed at by children on school buses. Those who perceive that they are considered the lowest rung of society's ladder may defend themselves by forming a street identity that lifts them above the impersonal label of "homeless" and helps them to make sense of their situation.

For example, each individual's reason for homelessness becomes a major part of their self-identity and sense of self-worth. Since few people claim to choose street life over a home and stability, the majority of street people increase their self-esteem by explaining their predicament. Willie told Snow and Anderson, "It ain't my fault I'm on the streets. I didn't choose to become homeless. I just had a lot of bad luck. And that ain't my fault." Willie's friend Ron says, "It wasn't my fault I lost my job in Denver. If I'd been working down the street, maybe I'd still be there. I was just at the wrong place at the wrong time. Like Willie said, some people just ain't got no luck!"

People who find themselves on the street for the first time are likely to fear the company of long-term street inhabitants. They are quick to say that they are not really homeless, that it is only a temporary setback. They are not bums, are not like the others in shelters or soup kitchens; they must stand in line only once, only today, until things get better. They try to disassociate themselves from people who may represent a mirror image of who they fear the most: themselves at their lowest, themselves without resources or hope. Tony told his Austin interviewers, "I'm not like the other guys who hang out down at the Sally. If you want to know about street people, I can tell you about them; but you can't really learn about street people from studying me, because I'm different."

After weeks or months on the streets, however, homeless men and women tend to lose sight of the secure world in which they once lived. They learn by observation how other street people survive. They drift into the fraternity of street life where their self-identity is now rooted and where they may gain acceptance from others who also happen to be down on their luck. Then their pride is centered in an oft-heard response to members of conventional society: "We're just like you."

Self-reliance

Some long-term homeless people build an identity around self-reliance. Cathy and Joe met on a park bench in New York City and married before they established their home in an alcove of the abandoned railway tunnel where they were interviewed by Margaret Morton. "I don't get welfare. Whatever I get out on the street is mine," Joe said. Cathy explained living in their underground home:

> We painted it, put in nice pillows and blankets and stuff like that—more color. He does the cooking. I clean, he cooks. No running water. That's it. Other than that, it's perfect. . . . You know, a lot of people have these ideas that we're living here

because we want to live here. We don't live here because we want to. It's the only place we got. We're not wanted upstairs [above ground]. You can't sleep on a park bench. You can't go anywhere. So this is what we got. People don't understand this. I make it the best way I know how. I don't steal. I don't panhandle. I just do what I have to do and that's it. That's it.

Spun tales of past and present successes also help form an individual's identity, as do fantasies about future plans for self-employment, lasting relationships, and the acquisition of money and possessions. Some people's stories are embellished, that is, stretched to make a partial reality sound better than it is. They may claim to work for high wages at jobs they really did hold in the past, explaining that they have been laid off, or are moving to a similar job, or that they were treated poorly by their employer and had to quit. An Austin panhandler bragged that he turned down a job paying $18.50 an hour; however, he told his story while he begged daily for spare change and cigarettes.

In the absence of jobs and money, other street people may build their identity on their beliefs, traditions, talents, or 12-step programs that they attend. Tanner, twenty-nine,

Cathy poses for a photograph inside the abandoned railway tunnel that is now her home. "We don't live here because we want to," Cathy explains, "it's the only place we got."

was described by his interviewers as literate and well-read, yet emotionally disturbed. After spending four months on the streets of Austin, he took to the road, saying he wanted to study at the Smithsonian in Washington, D.C. His self-identity focused on intelligence, underappreciated ability, and scholarship. He also claimed to be a prophet who could see into the future. Unlike street people who are able to form short-term friendships, Tanner was an outsider.

Friendships

Street people may form fleeting friendships with other homeless people. Thus, their self-identity is shaped in part by their ability to make friends. A street person named Marilyn told Snow and Anderson that she had "over 150 friends on the streets." She said that "us transients stick together."

Buddies and "best friends" who share food and sleeping quarters, who swap stories and plan joint futures, usually do not know their friend's real name. "Don't tell me your name," Marilyn said. "The first thing, I know your name, and then the police'll be coming around asking questions. I don't want to know names. I know faces." Marilyn, forty-nine, moved from Nova Scotia to West Virginia to Austin, where her street friends called her "Mom." Marilyn's friend Nona, forty-six, was a ten-year resident of Austin's streets; however, the Oklahoma woman gave a different name to police each time she was arrested. Thus, nicknames provide privacy and protection in the ever-hostile world of the street.

Street people also speak of betrayals by friends. Marilyn had a job that provided an efficiency apartment, and she had been off the streets for ten months.

> Then one day there's a knock on my door and here's three old friends who've just got in from San Antone. They asked if they could get showers and spend the night. Then, when I was at work, they ripped up my place and got in a fight out at the swimming pool, so I ended up losing my job and my apartment over that. That's why I'm back on the streets—'cause I tried to help some transients.

Some homeless people form attachments to animals. Cathy said of her animal friends, "I got my little family [eighteen cats], and that's enough. I don't need any more. They are all different, and if you're feeling bad they make you feel better. They're not like people, they're not two-faced. So that's why I love my animals. And they know they can depend on me."

Substance use and abuse

Some friendships form around the purchase and consumption of illegal drugs or alcohol. Drinking buddies pool their money to buy liquor for all to share. In addition to pooled resources such as money and shared drinking space—an abandoned car, for example—drinking buddies also rely on safety in numbers. Potential dangers such as robbery and arrest increase when a person is obviously drunk, drugged, or asleep on the street. As one Austin woman told Snow and Anderson, "If you get drunk alone, you're asking for it, but as long as you're with some people, no one's going to bother you."

Although substance abuse may reduce people to life on the streets, alcohol and drug use more frequently serve as a coping mechanism for enduring the boredom and trauma of living on the streets. In Austin, Marilyn said, "I didn't have much of a drinking problem before I landed on the streets. But I found it all so depressing. And everybody else was drinking and asking me to drink. So I said, 'Why not?' I mean, what did I have to lose? Everything was so depressing. Drinking sure couldn't make it any worse!" When Marilyn first landed on the streets, she was an occasional drinker. After two years on the streets, she drank regularly and more heavily. This pattern repeats itself in studies of the street homeless in various parts of the country. In general, the longer a person is homeless, the more frequently he or she tends to escape into the numbness of alcohol or other drugs. The older a person is, the more likely he or she is to turn to alcohol rather than to illegal drugs. Younger inhabitants of the street tend to favor crack cocaine and marijuana over alcohol. However, some homeless people report that they rarely or never drink alcohol or use illegal drugs. Some shun those who do.

Bernard, called Lord of the Tunnel by his friends, chased away the worst of the crack users from his underground neighborhood. He told Margaret Morton,

> Crack is really a fool's drug. It is. It is designed to create chaos—couldn't get no rest for a while because there was so much crack coming through. When something becomes chaotic, when something creates disturbances within your environment, it doesn't belong. When the environment suffers, changes have to be made. It's that simple.

Time on the streets

A homeless person's self-identity changes over time, depending on how long he or she lives on the streets. Those new to the street are reacting to the shock and horror of their situation. They do not know whom to trust, where to go, how to get help or find work, or how to survive among homeless strangers with whom they have not yet identified. They do not claim to be homeless, and they do not want to be associated with street people who brag about how long they have survived on the streets. Those new to the street are the ones most likely to seek and hold conventional jobs and day labor, and the most likely to rely on service providers such as the Salvation Army—for a while. Their hopes for financial recovery are high.

If they do not financially recover, if they are unable to get off the streets within the days, weeks, or months they expect, they slip into a new phase of street life: loss of ideals and personal direction, more identification with fellow street people, acquisition of new techniques for survival, and the tendency to take less action toward escaping the street. Time may become a blur of depression, inaction, and perhaps drug use as they walk the tightrope between memories of a home and an uncertain future.

As more time passes, street dwellers begin to focus more on surviving *on* the streets than on getting *off* the streets. Goals shift. Memories fade. They enter the society of homelessness and acknowledge that they belong to a social group that is set apart from conventional society. Now they take street life for granted. They lose their former self-identities and take on the group's identity. They don't look back, and they don't look forward. They live in the moment. They survive this morning, this afternoon, this evening.

After more years on the streets, they become less mobile. They tend to drink more and worry less. Physically or mentally ill from substance abuse and hardship, they no longer look for day labor. Instead, they scavenge, beg, and panhandle. If asked, the majority would not say that they chose their lifestyle but that it happened to them. They are quick to say how long they have survived on the street. For example, Banjo, forty-five, told Snow and Anderson that he ran away from home in Arkansas at sixteen to take a job with a carnival. Transient ever since, he travels around the country most of the year, and spends his winters in Austin. Shotgun, forty-nine, also winters in Austin. During fourteen of his years on the road, Shotgun did summer work at ranches in Montana. These long-term homeless men viewed their

Homeless people in Manhattan, New York, line up outside a local synagogue that serves breakfast to the needy. The newly homeless are the most likely to seek out service providers and charities.

years of survival as badges of fortitude. They had progressed through all the stages of homelessness, although their stays in various stages differed by months or years.

Daily routines

The daily routine of people on the street is similar to that of everyone else who wants to eat, sleep, earn, spend, exercise, play, make friends, and believe in one's self. A portion of each day is spent engaging in these activities. Unlike conventional society, however, exercise takes the form of moving from one source of help to another: from shelter to agency to another agency to promised work then back to the shelter, in pursuit of all other activities. Each person's daily routine is his or her unique map for navigating the subculture of street life. Some street people refer to their daily routine as "making the rounds."

Tunnel resident Bernard described to Margaret Morton how he made his aboveground rounds to fetch water, collect and sell cans, and harvest edible food discarded by restaurants and grocery stores. He illustrated his daily routine:

> Larry and I sat here the other day, and I made steamed cauliflower, wild rice, chicken. We're sittin' there listening to jazz—and a forty ounce of beer apiece. And I said, "Larry, this is too simple for most people." See, people think they gotta be out there, out there chasing the next hit of crack or whatever. You can bring everything you want to do right here. You have your food. When this is over with, you go to bed. Your days—what more could you ask for?

Work and resourcefulness

The daily challenge to survive persuades street people to be innovative and resourceful. Strategies include day labor; scavenging; panhandling; soliciting donations in public places; selling or trading junk, personal possessions, or stolen property; selling illegal goods and services; and theft.

Panhandlers—those who entertain passersby in exchange for money—look down on "bums" and "beggars." In the subculture of street life, playing music or reciting poetry is viewed as work. Begging is not. Beggars are at the bottom of the street's social ladder. Often ridiculed as crazy, these

A beggar holds his hand out, hoping passersby will give him money. Street people such as panhandlers look down on beggars because they do not work for their earnings.

types typically are mentally ill. Rhyming Mike, who earns his way by selling short poems to passersby, is a self-proclaimed street poet, although Austin's housed people might classify him as a panhandler.

Scavengers, or "dumpster divers," are successful if they can find food and supplies for themselves, as well as items for profit. Discarded clothing, jewelry, and tools can be pawned or sold. Items in "care packages" from relatives can be traded or sold for cash. The homeless trade and sell items among one another in the same way that people in conventional neighborhoods sell items at garage or yard sales. Ria, a tunnel resident interviewed by Morton, said, "I find stuff in the garbage cans and I sell it. Find an old piece of cloth, lay it on the street, put its junk there and just sell it. I made up to ninety dollars in one day. . . . I feel free. No bills. Nobody knocking on the door."

Gypsy Bill and Pushcart chose nicknames that proclaim their way of life. Gypsy Bill bragged that he was an "expert dumpster diver." Tunnel resident Bernard's cash source was aluminum can redemption. He told Morton, "Can redemption is probably the greatest thing that ever happened to the City in a long time. We go to We Can one day and you'll see that it's not just homeless people. I mean you have a lot of elderly people, people on fixed in-comes. It helps. It helps keep everything going."

A "dumpster diver" searches for aluminum cans in a garbage bin. Scavengers can make small profits by recycling cans and other items they find in the trash.

Arman Rahman's employment history reflects descending levels of work, from day labor to scavenging. According to *Village Voice,* when Arman left Bangladesh for New York City in 1991, he could not speak English. Therefore he was an easy target for employers who hire day laborers to demolish buildings, haul asbestos without permits, wash dishes, and dump table scraps. Living in dismal shared rooms, Arman worked three years for such employers. Then he moved into a three-by-eight-foot cardboard box beneath the Long Island Expressway, where he supports himself by selling bottles and cans. His microwave oven is powered by a scavenged automobile battery. He warms himself and cooks tea over outdoor wood fires. A makeshift pen protects his only friend: a rooster. Thus, work and ingenuity provide him with food, shelter, and companionship.

Drug dealing and prostitution

Drug dealing among transients is not the high-profit business that nontransient criminals engage in. A housed crack dealer profits by exploiting the addicted homeless who receive nothing for their money but a quick high.

However, a transient's illegal drugs are more likely to be bartered for another transient's alcohol, cigarettes, or snacks than to be sold for money. Likewise, a transient's scavenged jeans can be traded for the marijuana in another homeless person's pocket. Prostitution, on the other hand, is a money-making venture.

Prostitution among the homeless involves more men than women, and more young men than older men. However, interviews with the homeless indicate that the ratio of homosexual to heterosexual men mirrors the ratio in conventional, housed society. This means that homosexual prostitution thrives because it is profitable and because men outnumber women on the street. However, more common among homeless men or women is a brief sexual attachment to another man or woman in exchange for friendship and support.

In the street subculture, robbing a solicitor is often viewed as an admirable motive for prostitution. One man said after robbing his solicitor, "I split with his Caddy [Cadillac], a stereo, and a new TV and sold them on the streets for twenty-five hundred bucks." According to Snow and Anderson, success stories—enhanced and fabricated—abound on the street. Theft among themselves, however, is more common. Pushcart told Snow and Anderson that he justifies street theft this way: "I'll say, 'Hey, wake up! I'm gonna take your cans!' If he doesn't wake up, it's 'Sayonara.' Hey, it's happened to me. What goes around, comes around."

Plasma sales and day labor

Blood banks and plasma centers are legal and profitable sources of income. Plasma can be drawn from the blood twice per week without endangering the donor's health. In Austin, for example, plasma donors earn $8 for the first donation and $10 for the second donation within a week. The homeless view plasma donation as admirable work, since blood donors are helping the medical community and society overall. Unlike day labor, minimum-wage, or shift work, plasma donation provides guaranteed income rather than false or short-lived promises.

The job corner and the labor pool may vary by name from city to city, but they are the primary means for the homeless to find traditional work, as well as transportation to and from the job. Unfortunately, unscrupulous employers exist, and street people take their chances when they sign on with any employer willing to hire transients. Marilyn related her experience with such an employer to interviewers Snow and Anderson:

> We went and worked on this job a week. The boss said he'd pay us at the end of the week. We were there the day he got $2,500. And he took us to the Tamale House and said he was going to go to the bank and cash the check and come back and pay us, but he never came back and nobody got their money. See, he was a subcontractor and there was four of us working for him. He said he was paying each one of us $5 an hour. But none of us got paid and nobody's ever seen him around since.

Hopes and plans for the future

Those who say they are down on their luck often expect their luck to turn, especially if their luck has been bad for a long time. A belief that life will get better constitutes the life plan for street people who perceive that they have "paid their dues" and deserve better. Gypsy Bill, for example, told Snow and Anderson that he expected to come into some money. Although he could not imagine the source of the money, he said, "You may think I'm crazy, but it's this feeling I've got. Besides, I deserve it 'cause I've paid my dues."

Hoyt Page told Snow and Anderson, "I've been down on my luck for so long, it's got to change. . . . Like I said before, I believe what goes around, comes around, so I'm due a run of good luck, don't you think?" Shotgun explained, "I been on the streets for about fifteen years. . . . I rode the boxcars and slept out in the wintertime. That's how you pay your dues." These men typify long-time residents of the street who believe that their future is forecast by luck, by paying their dues, and by waiting for what goes around to come around.

Others lay elaborate plans for the future. Three street buddies, interviewed by Snow and Anderson, had met for the first time hours earlier, yet claimed to be close

Although street friendships enhance a homeless person's situation, most of the homeless long for the time when they will be off the streets.

friends. They planned to hitchhike to St. Louis, stay with one of their families for a while, then find jobs and rent an apartment together. One of the three, a younger man, assured an older of the three, "No one's gonna beat you up when I'm around. I guarantee you that." Hours later, the three had separated: one to sleep behind a retaining wall, one to a hobo jungle in South Austin, and the third to eat dinner at the Salvation Army. The friendship, and the plan, had disintegrated.

Awaiting sleep on the hard floor of a winter shelter, a Pittsburgh transient told Snow and Anderson, "Tomorrow morning I'm going to get my money . . . catch a plane to Pittsburgh and tomorrow night I'll take a hot bath, have a dinner of linguine and red wine in my own restaurant, and have a woman hanging on my arm." The next night he explained why he was still in Austin: "I've been informed that all my money is tied up in a legal battle back in Pittsburgh."

Hopes and plans to get off the street may begin as tall tales, daydreams, a means of elevating one's self-esteem, or a genuine hunger for partnership and friendship. And, in the dangerous and degrading social system in which street people exist, such a plan may be nothing more than self-delusion.

4

Homeless Children

FOR MANY OF the street people interviewed by David A. Snow and Leon Anderson, homelessness is a way of life that began in childhood. For example, Hoyt Page was thirty-seven when he described his early descent into homelessness. Orphaned as a child, he was passed from one relative to another and finally to an orphanage, where at the age of thirteen he strangled a boy who was ridiculing Hoyt as a bed wetter. This incident branded him a juvenile delinquent and resulted in his transfer from the orphanage to a correctional institution. After his release, he joined the army. A few years later he joined the subculture of the street, and he has lived on the road ever since. His 6'6" frame and his drug-and-alcohol-ravaged face mask his beginnings as a homeless child. And, whereas he had a roof over his head throughout his childhood, some might question whether he was ever a homeless child at all. Today, as then, homeless children and youth are often difficult to find and define.

Identifying homeless children

Children who accompany homeless family members to shelters are easily labeled and counted as homeless. However, murky definitions separate runaways, street kids, pushouts, throwaways, and the homeless. When children under the age of eighteen leave home, their reasons for leaving may be hard to determine. Even if children are reported missing by people with whom they lived or by other concerned adults, authorities cannot always determine whether a child ran away, was abducted, or was evicted—pushed out—by a family member. Children who leave home with no alternative place to stay, yet who have parental permission to leave, may be labeled as throwaways or castaways, since their parents have relinquished responsibility for their well-being. As long ago as 1983, the U.S. Department of Health and Human Services defined "street kids" as youths who believe they belong on the street and have become accustomed to fending for themselves. Even the 1990 census did not separate homeless children from homeless adolescents, nor did it identify how many children and adolescents are homeless and on their own.

Many homeless children and adolescents are runaways—who have opted to leave their homes—or throwaways —who have been forced onto the streets by their families.

The 1990 census count—taken on national "Shelter Night"—found nearly 29,000 children under the age of eighteen in emergency shelters and about 5,600 in shelters for abused women. Although 10,000 individuals were counted in runaway and children's shelters, and nearly 50,000 individuals were counted as visible homeless in street locations, no distinction was made regarding the age of these individuals or whether they were with a responsible adult. The census also found 104,200 individuals in juvenile institutions, but these institutions are not categorized either. Thus another murky definition separates homeless children from those who reside in correctional facilities and orphanages. For children without families, an orphanage is a form of home, yet it does not typify the most common definition of home: the family dwelling.

Even young people without homes categorize themselves in a variety of ways. When residents of New York City youth shelters were asked if they considered themselves as a runaway or as homeless, 44 percent labeled themselves runaways, 34 percent labeled themselves as homeless, and 22 percent said they were both.

Unaccompanied youth

After the Census Bureau released its 1990 figures, advocacy groups and organizations attempted to more clearly identify homeless children and adolescents. The U.S. Conference of Mayors estimated in 1995 that "unaccompanied youth" represented 3.5 percent of the homeless population in America's twenty-nine major cities. This estimate shows an increase from 3 percent in 1990. The National Coalition for the Homeless estimated in 1996 that 300,000 street adolescents have no positive supervision from a parent or responsible adult. However, this estimate does not differentiate between homeless adolescents and those who may be on the street for a short while before they return home. Nor does it separate throwaways from runaways.

Until 1974, runaways were considered juvenile delinquents. That is, running away from home was considered a crime for which the runaway could be arrested and jailed.

The Runaway and Homeless Youth Act of 1974 relaxed the laws that punish runaways. However, street adolescents typically survive by panhandling, drug dealing, shoplifting, and prostitution, which are punishable crimes. Thus, if homeless adolescents engage in illegal activities, they risk being arrested.

Many so-called runaways are literally running away from dangerous situations at home: physical and sexual abuse or caretakers who are engaged in illegal activities such as drug dealing. On the run and alone, these teens may hide from authorities who would return them to their families or place them in foster care or orphanages. For example, fifteen-year-old S. W. described his homelessness to counselors at Stepping Stone, a youth crisis shelter in California: "My mother [as a child] got stripped and tied to her bed and beaten by her father and grandfather. So when I was growing up my mother thought that was the way a child should be raised." S. W.'s male relatives abused him sexually. He ran away. After moving in with a stranger who forced him to deal drugs in exchange for shelter, he returned to his mother in California. Next he attempted suicide. While hospitalized, he was offered foster home placement. He declined. "I stayed at the Tom Bradley Terminal, Los Angeles Airport . . . for about 5 days." A few weeks later, he found refuge, work, and a future as a peer counselor at Stepping Stone.

Children of homeless parents

Children of homeless parents are easier to identify than are unaccompanied youth. According to Homes for the Homeless, the typical homeless family consists of a twenty-year-old single mother and two children under the age of six. The mother is unlikely to have completed high school or to have held a job. Chances are one in four that she grew up in foster care. If so, her children are twice as likely as other homeless children to be abused or neglected and four times more likely to drop out of school. Such statistics inspired Homes for the Homeless president Ralph da Costa Nunez to say, "Homelessness is not a

A homeless child sleeps on a sidewalk in Harrisburg, Pennsylvania. Homeless children are often developmentally delayed and suffer from a variety of behavior problems due to their lifestyle.

housing issue; it is an education issue, a children's issue, and a family issue."

A growing number of today's homeless children represent the third generation to grow up within a cycle of inadequate education, domestic violence, substance abuse, joblessness, homelessness, and poverty. "When I was seventeen I got pregnant, dropped out of school, and moved in with my boyfriend," Anna told her counselor at America's Family Inns. "After a few years I became so afraid of his beatings that I took my two children and moved out. I was all alone and unable to get a job. I haven't seen my dad since he left my mother when I was seven, so I can't turn to him for help and my mom kicked me out when I had my first baby." Thus, Anna's children are the homeless children of a homeless mother who herself was a teenage throwaway. Anna's children have witnessed domestic violence, as have about half of all homeless children. And Anna's children—along with more than 40 percent of all homeless children—have been homeless more than once; Anna was homeless for the third time when she told her story.

Developmental delays

As a result of the destructive cycle in which homeless children live, they suffer physically, emotionally, socially, and developmentally. According to Dr. Ellen Bassuk of

Harvard Medical School, homeless preschoolers display a wide range of serious emotional, social, and cognitive problems. Standardized tests that measure developmental milestones showed that 47 percent of the children she tested had a delay in either language, gross motor skills (walking, for example), fine motor coordination (such as building a simple tower of blocks), or personal and social development (drinking from a cup, for example). A third of the children had delays in two or more of these areas. Although children who live in extreme poverty often exhibit delays in language development, multiple delays are unusual. Dr. Bassuk believes that the stress of losing one's home combined with the stress of shelter life intensifies existing delays and causes others.

Dr. Bassuk shares the story of thirteen-month-old William, whose parents abused drugs before his birth. After William's father went to prison, his mother quit her job, escaped her depression by relying on alcohol, and was evicted for nonpayment of rent. When William was tested at the shelter where he and his mother lived, the preschooler could not stand or walk. He spoke no distinguishable words. Like many other homeless preschoolers, William showed developmental delays in all four areas of testing.

Emotional problems

After children arrive at a shelter, they exhibit more behavioral problems than housed children. Homeless preschoolers observed in New York day-care centers showed regressive behaviors, lack of inhibitions with strangers, and immature relationships with peers. Increased hyperactive behavior seemed to be a way to cope with a cramped environment.

According to Andrea Solarz of the American Psychological Association, the sudden withdrawal or aggression exhibited by sheltered children indicates high levels of stress and distress. Said one sheltered mother, "There is a life that goes on in the shelters that a lot of people never see, and that is depression." Another sheltered mother said, "My youngest daughter has internalized her anger. She is extremely

A toddler examines pieces of rock and wood while playing outside his shanty. Although many homeless parents provide adequate care for their children, a large number of homeless youth are the victims of abuse and neglect.

depressed. She was very ashamed to tell people where she lived [at the shelter], so she didn't make friends at school."

Dr. Bassuk's study showed that half the sheltered school-age children she tested needed further psychiatric evaluation. Almost all said they had thought of suicide. Depression and stress also hindered their ability to learn. Bassuk describes Martha, a six-year-old who was sexually abused by her mother's boyfriend before she and her mother entered a shelter. "I used to know my ABCs," Martha said in the shelter, "but I can't remember them anymore." The child psychologist who evaluated Martha determined that the little girl was in an emotional crisis that might require hospitalization. She was clingy, demanding, preoccupied with her body, and cried for long periods of time. Before she could be hospitalized, shelter workers discovered that Martha's mother was abandoning her at the shelter—to be cared for by other homeless mothers—or was allowing the abusive boyfriend to pick Martha up after school. Social service workers came to the shelter, took Martha away, and placed her in foster care. She was described, at that time, as traumatized.

Abuse and neglect

The trauma of homelessness affects the whole family, and may place homeless children at greater risk of abuse or neglect than children who are not homeless. Not all impoverished or homeless parents abuse or neglect their children, however. Unlike Martha's mother, not all homeless parents hand over their children to an abusive adult or to strangers in a shelter. Opinions vary as to why combinations of factors lead to abuse in some families, while other families cope with stress in healthier ways. One theory is that women who suffer from low self-esteem tolerate abuse more readily than women who believe they can enact positive change in their lives by escaping their abuser and living on their own. Abused women, and children who are abused or neglected by their caregivers, exhibit a hopelessness that is compounded when they become homeless.

Sociologist Kay Young McChesney interviewed Vangie, whose family moved from rural Mississippi to Los Angeles when Vangie was eight. Because her mother did not work, "she couldn't afford to send me back [to Mississippi] but she felt in her heart she couldn't afford to keep me." Then the abuse started.

> I would go to an arcade, or I would go to a park, just watching people. Sometimes I would cry because I hurt all over. I was ashamed to come to school with bruises on my body. One day I just went to school—I was sitting in the classroom. My body was hurting so bad that I just broke out crying, you know. The teacher said, "What's wrong with you?" I lifted my shirt, and I had extension cord marks on me. They called the police and my mother explained to the police, "Yes, I spanked my child 'cause she's mine, and I will spank her again."

No one interceded on Vangie's behalf. When Vangie was fourteen, her mother said, "Can't take it no more—get out." Vangie got out.

She lived in a local park until she was arrested for breaking curfew laws. Police photographed her beating scars and sent her to a detention facility. From there she moved into her first foster home where "the man [foster father] would come to molest me. I would tell people and no one believed me. 'You're a liar,' he said. . . . 'You're gonna be punished for this!'" Vangie ran back to the streets, was arrested again, and placed in another foster home. After that, she was "in and out" of foster homes, girls' homes, and on the streets. She became pregnant while living on the streets and was placed in a home for pregnant teenagers. When she decided to keep her daughter, they were both discharged to the streets. She was seventeen.

Vangie's story is typical of children who are abused at home, abused in foster care, and escape to a life on the streets. When she finally landed in a shelter, Vangie was twenty years old and functionally illiterate. Her résumé could list only shoplifting and prostitution—her means of support on the street. Out of touch with her family, alone, and temporarily sheltered, Vangie described her two-and-a-half-year-old daughter Randy as her "only reason for living."

Chronic health problems

According to the *American Journal of Public Health*, homeless children are twice as likely as children in general to experience chronic health problems. Their immunization records are often incomplete or missing. As a result of environmental exposure and unsanitary living conditions, homeless children are especially vulnerable to illnesses such as respiratory and ear infections, gastrointestinal problems, and lice infestations. Homeless children tested in New York City had higher blood concentrations of lead than did housed children who live in poverty. When children enter a shelter,

A homeless family has dinner on a bench outside of the nation's capitol. Homeless children are often forced to go days without food, resulting in malnutrition and other maladies.

they become susceptible to disease transmission and inadequate personal hygiene associated with living in close quarters with others. Homeless infants are especially at risk when caregivers lack refrigeration for milk or formula.

Homeless children also experience more dental problems than housed children, more nutritional deficiencies, and the ironic combination of hunger and obesity. In welfare motels where cooking is not allowed, families may eat one meal a day in a fast-food restaurant. In such situations, hunger and obesity go hand in hand. According to the Urban Institute, the homeless eat fewer meals each day than average Americans, and often go entire days without food. Although shelters and emergency food assistance centers attempt to provide nutritionally balanced meals, residency turnover rates are high. The healthy meals a child eats while in a shelter cannot compensate for long periods of inadequate food and poor nutrition.

When homeless children get sick, they will likely be treated in a hospital emergency room rather than a public or private clinic. Lack of money or insurance coverage prevents parents from seeking medical or dental care until symptoms escalate into an emergency. A San Diego survey found that 56 percent of recently homeless parents had no source of health care, and almost half had no form of health insurance. And when children move from one temporary residence to another, they are unlikely to receive follow-up care after their health emergency subsides.

Dr. Marjorie J. Robertson reports that homeless adolescents are subject to high rates of malnutrition, sexually transmitted disease, sexual and physical assault, and murder. Findings published in the *American Journal of Public Health* show that homeless youths at a Los Angeles medical clinic displayed higher rates of heart conditions, kidney failure, pneumonia, hepatitis, trauma, and rape than did housed youths served by the same clinic.

Damaged family relationships

NCH reports that homelessness frequently breaks up families. When parents become homeless, their children may be placed in foster care. Some homeless parents leave their children with friends or family to protect them from abuse, street life, or hardship in an emergency shelter. Some shelter policies deny access to older boys or fathers. Other shelters are designated for use by adults only. During a survey in New York City's singles-only shelters, 60 percent of the residents had children who had been placed elsewhere. In Maryland, only 43 percent of parents living in shelters had their children with them. And in a Chicago survey, 91 percent of sheltered and unsheltered parents did not have their children with them at the time they were interviewed.

Inappropriate role expectations also add stress to a child's life. Homeless mothers describe how they are supported by their children during hard times. Beth was bedridden in a shelter with her ten-year-old daughter Daisy. "Daisy was worried about me," Beth said. "She cleaned my sores. My [surgical] incision abscessed, and as much as I tried to wash it when I was in the shower, she'd say, 'Mama, it's O.K. I'll do it.' She took care of me." Susan said of her six-year-old daughter Terry, "I think probably we helped each other. Who knows where I would have been if I hadn't had her, I mean emotionally. I may never have come out of it."

School failure

More than any other activity, school attendance and related school activities consume most of every child's waking hours. Absence from school or withdrawal from school forecasts failure and financial struggle in the years ahead. Therefore, attendance in school is among the most important issues facing homeless children.

When homelessness among families gained media attention in the 1980s, activists publicized the barriers encountered by school-age children when enrolling in school. In those days, schools required a permanent address, birth certificate and immunization records, proof of guardianship, and transfers of permanent records before a child could officially enroll. Homeless children on the move or in shelters faced discrimination simply for being homeless. Furthermore, as families moved from one school district to

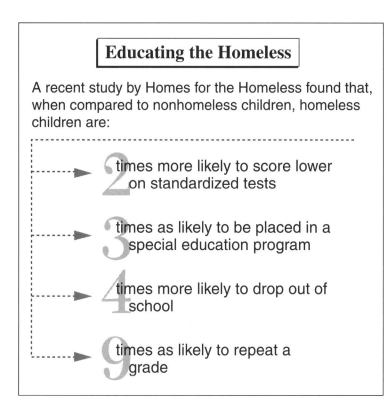

Educating the Homeless

A recent study by Homes for the Homeless found that, when compared to nonhomeless children, homeless children are:

2 times more likely to score lower on standardized tests

3 times as likely to be placed in a special education program

4 times more likely to drop out of school

9 times as likely to repeat a grade

another—often because city shelters limited the length of a family's stay—children suffered the instability of constant change. Their self-esteem suffered when peers ridiculed their homelessness and their tendency to fail. Shelters offered no privacy or quiet space for homework. According to NCH, as many as 50 percent of homeless children attended school irregularly in the mid-1980s.

Of the school-age children tested by Dr. Ellen Bassuk, 43 percent had repeated a grade. One-fourth were in special or remedial classes. Two teenage brothers she interviewed were so ashamed of their homelessness that they kept it a secret at school. Michael and Tommy avoided making friends and did not confide in their teachers. They invented telephone numbers and lied about the address of the welfare motel where they had been living for a year and a half. The boys began to skip school. Both had to repeat a grade. Prior to becoming homeless, Michael and Tommy had been average students. In addition to school failures, the brothers also scored high on a test for anxiety and depression.

Education and the McKinney Act

The 1987 Stewart B. McKinney Homeless Assistance Act required all fifty states to take steps that would guarantee all homeless children the same right to a "free and appropriate public education" as housed children. Barriers were lifted. For example, the McKinney Act made it illegal to bar enrollment to a student who has no permanent address. In 1990, Congress amended the McKinney Act, specifying that states would not only enroll homeless children, but would promote their academic success by developing and providing programs that serve the educational, social, and health needs of homeless children. The McKinney Act allocated funds to pay for such services as tutoring, health and dental screening, and after-school enrichment. Another amendment in 1994 broadened McKinney funds to provide similar services for preschool children. Under the act's guidelines, schools are also directed to comply with homeless parents' requests to enroll a child in a particular school. In many cases, schools must provide students' transportation to the selected schools.

A homeless nine-year-old reviews her homework with her mother as they sit in the cafeteria of a homeless shelter.

Within a decade, the McKinney Act provided constructive change for homeless families. The National Association of State Coordinators for the Education of Homeless Children and Youth reports that average school attendance in 1995 was at 86 percent, representing a 66 percent increase since 1987. McKinney programs served 275,000 homeless children and youth in thirty-three states, wherein at least 520 local education agencies received McKinney grants. However, service providers and shelter operators say students still need greater access to special education evaluations and services, before- and after-school care programs, and after-school events. NCH stated in 1997 that about 18 percent of homeless students do not attend school and that transportation continues to be the greatest challenge facing homeless children.

Accomplishments and challenges

After the McKinney Act forced states to examine how they educate homeless children, perceptions about homelessness changed. For example, teachers in Columbia, South Carolina, volunteered at Sister Care Center for abused mothers in order to learn new ways to address the special needs of homeless students in their classes. After discovering that a majority of the families had very young children, one teacher set up a study area at the shelter, visited with parents, and served as a liaison between homeless families and school counselors. Another developed a mentoring relationship with a middle school student, checking with him often to see how he and his family were doing. Another volunteer realized that homeless children "must spend much energy just on survival issues. I'll think twice before responding too quickly to a homeless student's failure to do homework."

The National Association of State Coordinators for the Education of Homeless Children and Youth reports that other states are also earning high marks in educating homeless children. In 1996 New York funded programs for 22,000 homeless children in forty-four locales. In New York City, the Cultural Arts Program for children in temporary housing provided on-site instruction in literature, the sciences, or the visual and performing arts at cultural institutions throughout the city. Life-skills classes elsewhere taught the importance of attending school and planning for higher-level education. Mississippi sent the Mobile Classroom to shelters in the Natchez area, ran a camp for Starkville children between the ages of five and thirteen, and provided a summer transition program to help children prepare for kindergarten.

In rural areas, local school agencies must devise ingenious ways to reach homeless children. South Dakota, for example, is challenged by its vast, rural terrain. Of its 3,270 homeless children, only about 10 percent were served by McKinney funds in 1996. However, the state coordinator broadcast public service announcements on radio and television to encourage homeless children to enroll and stay in school. Nebraska, also vast and sparsely populated, served only 793 of its 5,600 homeless children even though its largest cities, Omaha and Lincoln, transported students from shelters, hotels, and motels to their school of origin (their school before they became homeless).

As these programs illustrate, America's educators are attempting to address the unique needs of homeless children, whether urban or rural. As a result, homeless children in all fifty states have benefited from services paid for with McKinney grants. Unfortunately, states applied for grants and initiated services because McKinney legislation required states to act. Although states must still address the needs of homeless schoolchildren according to McKinney legislation, the 1996 federal budget reduced McKinney grants by 20 percent. This means that unless states choose to make up the loss by using taxpayer dollars, existing programs will suffer after 1997.

In Iowa, for example, 1,350 homeless children were served in 1994–1995 out of a total of 9,900 homeless children in the state. A decade ago, state educators counted only 4,129 homeless children and youth in Iowa. Educators and service providers fear that McKinney budget cuts will not only diminish existing programs but will drastically reduce the possibility that Iowa will be able to help its increasing number of homeless children. Iowa's concerns echo those heard throughout the fifty states.

5

The Shelter System

ALTHOUGH THE FEDERAL government requires states to provide educational opportunities for homeless children, there is no federal policy requiring states or localities to provide uniform systems of shelter for the homeless. Therefore, local governments and private charities operate shelter systems that vary widely from place to place. Some communities do not have shelter systems that meet short-term emergency needs of the transient homeless or provide extended housing for youth or families or victims of domestic violence. Some communities have no shelters at all. Thus, the unique situation that leads to each person's homelessness coexists with the unique response each person will experience when he or she seeks shelter.

Allocations and accommodations

The Department of Housing and Urban Development (HUD) is primarily responsible for federal programs for the homeless. McKinney funds support seventeen programs that HUD and other federal agencies oversee. About 80 percent of all McKinney funds are awarded according to the programs' guidelines, and they are designated for urgent needs such as food and shelter. However, since McKinney monies are typically awarded to states that provide matching funds, more money is authorized by Congress each year than is applied for, allocated, and spent. Since the use of McKinney funds is left to the discretion of each state, this means that funding to build a shelter may come from one fund, money for operating costs from another,

Children color and play soccer in the recreation room of a homeless shelter. State and local governments, as well as private charities, offer a variety of shelters for the homeless.

and money for staff from a third. Services falter when there is a lack of coordination between HUD and local government. For example, if federal and state dollars pay for additional shelter beds, but city funds for counselors are reduced, homeless people may not receive the counseling they need in order to move beyond the immediate emergency of homelessness.

Services for the homeless in Los Angeles County, California, vary by jurisdiction. By 1991, the county, as well as the municipalities of Los Angeles, Long Beach, and Santa Monica—four jurisdictions in all—had individual policies and services for the homeless. Allocations came from the federal government, the state of California general fund, and the Los Angeles County general fund. Some of the cities pooled their resources to support existing, privately operated shelters. The county, along with some of the cities within the county, also set up inclement weather shelters paid for with federal funds.

Nearby, but outside the county, West Hollywood and Pasadena set their own public policies. West Hollywood and Santa Monica enforced anticamping ordinances, while Pasadena funded new programs. Meanwhile, the administrator of another nearby municipality said, "Our City would like to do something to help the homeless, but . . . frankly we don't want to end up being a magnet for homeless people and have things get out of control."

Communities with greater numbers of homeless people than their neighboring communities are typically those that have made a commitment to providing shelter and services. Experienced homeless people know where they are welcome, so that is where they go. Nationwide, the lack of uniform shelter systems is most challenging to people who are homeless for the first time and thus do not know where to turn for help. They may find that the type of shelter they need is not available in their neighborhood or in their town.

Finding shelter

When families or individuals are homeless for the first time, they are likely to call local government officials, a church or synagogue, or a homeless hot line telephone number for advice about what to do. States and large cities have task forces that are established to steer people toward the type of help they need, as well as to gather and share information about homelessness and homeless services in their locality. Although task forces cannot legislate policy that affects the homeless, they do attempt to coordinate state, local, and private efforts.

In Atlanta, Georgia, for example, the Atlanta Task Force for the Homeless is a twenty-four-hour emergency placement facility and central clearinghouse for homeless people in the city and the eight surrounding counties that make up metropolitan Atlanta. The Task Force for the Homeless is a nonprofit agency, funded in part by a $997,500 HUD grant designed to create nine hundred more shelter beds in metro Atlanta. Its employees work as shelter coordinators with about thirty independent agencies and service providers. Staff members advise callers of nightly or weekly fees at some of the area's shelters and of the lengthy application and evaluation process they will face at other area shelters. Each person who requests shelter is provided with an explanation of what types of shelter are available.

Types of shelter

Emergency shelters, also called short-term shelters, house people for a night, or a few nights, to several months. Long-term shelters provide transitional housing for several months to two years while people attempt to make the transition between homelessness and permanent housing. The terms *public, private,* and *specific-use* also identify types of shelter.

Public shelters are maintained by local governments with federal, state, or local funds or a combination of government funds. New York City has invested millions of dollars in its public shelter system in which about 6,000 homeless families live. In that city, all homeless families must first register at an emergency assistance unit (EAU) before they can enter a city shelter. Each month, over 700 new families wait in an EAU until they are assigned space in a shelter.

Private shelters are run by benevolent societies, service organizations, privately funded charities, and religious bodies such as the Salvation Army. Although McKinney legislation allots hundreds of millions of dollars for emergency services nationwide, HUD reports that 90 percent of all homeless shelters are privately operated. Therefore, private shelters provide about 80 percent of all shelter beds.

Although state and local task forces may encourage private groups to maintain specific standards for operating facilities, private groups are free to manage their shelters according to their own guidelines. However, if a private shelter receives federal funds to maintain a federal program for its residents, the shelter must abide by federal guidelines for that program.

Space permitting, some public shelter systems pledge to house everyone who requests shelter. Private shelters, on the other hand, may reserve the right to deny admission to any homeless person who does not conform to shelter policies. For example, shelters may bar admission to anyone who appears to be combative, high on drugs or alcohol, or who threatens the comfort and safety of other homeless residents or the staff. Thus, a first-time homeless person who walks into a shelter will discover that a bed is assigned according to the rules of the house. Experienced homeless people know that the rules vary from shelter to shelter.

Specific-use shelters house people whose homelessness can be categorized. Beds in specific-use shelters are reserved for battered women, the mentally ill, runaway youth, pregnant teens, men in recovery from substance abuse, women in recovery, youth in recovery, and combinations such as abused women in recovery with children. Family housing labeled as welfare hotels and motels are short-term, specific-use, public shelters where families receiving welfare benefits are placed.

Some private and specific-use shelters honor the individuality of each family. For example, Family Haven and Community-In-Partnership, two shelters operated by the Salvation Army in St. Louis, provide separate quarters for

A woman dines in the cafeteria of Haven of Hope, a specific-use shelter for homeless women who suffer from emotional problems.

two-parent families, for single males with children, for single females with children, for families with teenagers, and for extended families, such as grandparents with their children and grandchildren.

Availability

After learning what shelter options exist, a homeless person must find an available bed. If homeless for the first time, he or she may discover that the nearest shelter within walking distance is designated specific-use, or that the nearest short-term emergency shelter is miles away, or that a bed is not available in the type of shelter he or she needs.

For example, an abused older woman in Pittsburgh's East End will discover that her neighborhood's only emergency shelter is the House of the Good Samaritan. Its thirty-eight beds are reserved for men. East End also quarters Bill's House for homeless men with children, the East End Cooperative Ministry (men only), and the Whale's Tale Bridge Housing Program for people in recovery pro-

At drop-in shelters like this one in New York City, homeless patrons may be charged a minimal nightly fee for their stay.

grams. All are transitional housing programs. Womansplace admits abused women, but their shelters are uptown and in McKeesport. The YWCA of Greater Pittsburgh houses domestic violence victims, but they are at full capacity whenever they have twelve residents. In Southside, H.E.A.R.T. House has rooms for five families of women with children, but none for single, abused women. As this example illustrates, the problem of being homeless can be compounded by the frustration of trying to find available shelter and then finding transportation to that shelter.

Atlanta's Task Force reports a local shortage in emergency, short-term housing for people without any financial resources. Of 3,400 beds available year round in 1996 (3,800 beds in winter), many were specific-use beds. Shelter space for women with children is also limited. The Task Force helps 1,500 to 3,000 homeless people every month. More than 40,000 different individuals per year spend at least one night in the Atlanta shelter system, wherein only a third of all shelter space is available without barriers.

Barriers to shelter

Barriers include nightly or weekly fees, lengthy application or evaluation procedures, limited lengths of stay, and contracts requiring a percentage of the sheltered person's welfare or income. Public or private drop-in shelters such as those run by the Salvation Army charge no fee or a minimal fee. However, even a minimal nightly or weekly fee constitutes a barrier for people who arrive at a shelter without a cent in their pocket. People with no government benefits or no income must rely on free shelters.

Restrictions on length of stay vary from shelter to shelter. Shelter systems are designed to assist people with housing emergencies. Ideally, how long a person remains in the shelter system corresponds with how long it takes the person to resolve their emergency and return to permanent housing. Although a city's total number of shelter beds may equal or exceed the number of applicants for emergency shelter on a given night, length of stay in each shelter is usually limited from a few nights to several weeks or months. In some cities, cheap motels and hotels designated for homeless families limit a family's stay to a maximum of forty-five days. Families in transitional housing are usually awaiting Section 8 approval. If, during the wait, a transitional family fails to meet its lease agreement for income-percentage rent, or fails to keep a job or attend school as some leases require, the family will be evicted, only to return to emergency shelter where their length of stay will be limited.

Race and family size may also erect barriers to shelter and transitional housing. A 1993 study of homeless families in St. Louis revealed that for each additional child in a homeless family, the likelihood of finding permanent housing decreased, and white families were almost twice as likely as African American families to move from a shelter to permanent housing. However, 85 percent of the families were African American. Of these, 90 percent were mothers with children. These families tended to be larger than the white families, but only 13.5 percent of multifamily units had three or more bedrooms to accommodate larger families. In addition to its lack of adequate housing for large families, St. Louis was rated in 1994 as the eleventh most segregated city among 318 metropolitan areas. Housing resource workers in the mid-1980s reported little success in trying to place homeless black families in Section 8 units in some sections of St. Louis. Black families housed there were said to be "hounded out"—forced by other families to leave.

Navigating the system

Another barrier may arise when a homeless person tries to obtain housing, food, and support services within the same shelter or neighborhood. In single room occupancy housing (SROs) and welfare hotels where kitchens are nonexistent, residents must obtain food elsewhere. To apply for government benefits, shelter residents must travel to the agency's office. Work and educational requirements contingent on housing add other steps to take. Unless a shelter provides beds, food, clothing, medical services, so-

cial services, child care, and education—and a rare few do provide all—its residents must learn to navigate a system of service providers. For inexperienced homeless people, learning how to navigate the system can be as disheartening as losing one's home.

Most SROs and welfare hotel rooms lack kitchens, forcing residents to seek out other service providers for their meals.

A Los Angeles complainant told Legal Aid about her runaround difficulty:

> They gave me a voucher to a hotel in Huntington Park called the Longfellow. I didn't know where any of these places were, the unemployment office, the Social Security office, or anything. The worker told me the offices were downtown. She gave me nine bus tokens; that was supposed to last a whole week. I asked for food stamps for some way to eat. She said I didn't have the right kind of identification. So I had to go to the Longfellow to register by 5:00 P.M., otherwise I'd get locked out. The next day, since I didn't get food stamps, I had to go to one of the missions [5.5 miles away].

When Frances and her nine-year-old daughter Ellen phone-searched for family shelter in California's San Gabriel Valley, she learned that two beds were available—

downtown, twenty miles away, where she would have to be interviewed before admittance. "All I could think," she said, "[was] what am I gonna do? I'm broke, my clothes are in Pomona, I've got the clothes on my back, my child's got the clothes on her back. I've got no money, no place to go, no transportation." With darkness descending, Frances also feared that if she were denied admittance after the interview, she and her daughter would be stranded in the inner city at nightfall. She feared for their safety. Fortunately, a shelter worker heard Frances's fears and agreed to admit Frances and Ellen unconditionally upon arrival. Frances borrowed bus money from her sister and made it to the shelter before dark.

Sensitive and insensitive staff

In addition to performing their required duties, caring staff members and service providers may go out of their

A math teacher in a Pennsylvania shelter works with homeless residents who are trying to improve their skills. Caring shelter employees can have a positive influence in the lives of shelter residents.

way to help people negotiate the system. Jane, homeless in Los Angeles, said,

> The lady from Protective Services did something, went over somebody's head. "This lady needs money right away." And that lady, bless her heart, she gave me and my kids a hundred dollars, her own personal check, out of her own account. . . . The night they took my children away, up until now she's been the worker, and she's been through this little struggle with me, from place to place to place.

Elizabeth Lindsey, professor of social work at the University of North Carolina at Greensboro, believes that families cannot make the transition from homelessness to permanent housing without the help of individuals within the agencies and institutions that are designed to serve them. Lindsey writes of Georgia mothers who credit shelter staff with helping them acquire furniture, household goods, clothes, transportation, help in moving into new homes, and overall restabilization. One such mother, Mandy, said shelter staff were primarily responsible for her family's securing permanent housing because "they are the ones that hooked me up with the resources . . . and they're there to talk if you had a problem." Ellie said of her shelter's staff, "They helped me to put confidence in myself. They were there for me when I needed someone. . . . Without their encouragement and their push and . . . helping me to have confidence in myself, and the firmness, I wouldn't have ever made it."

However, not all homeless people are pleased with shelter staff or with individuals within agencies designed to help the homeless. For example, Jane felt abandoned by the system after her purse, which held her welfare money, was stolen in a Los Angeles shelter. She reported the theft to her caseworker, whose skepticism added to Jane's frustration and anger at being robbed.

> I think everything would go smoothly at the Department of Social Services if they treated you like a client and not like some tramp on the street. I'm not the type of person [like] these women that's just on drugs and spend their whole welfare check on things they're not supposed to. . . . You're just a set of numbers to those people. That's all you are. You're not

human. You're not supposed to have any feelings. If you do, you better put them on the bottom of your feet, and that's it.

Living conditions

Theft is one of many stressful experiences reported by homeless people in shelters. Most emergency shelters are large, impersonal places where one's sense of self is assaulted by the shouts, tears, tantrums, curses, and odors of dozens of people sleeping on cots in the same room. *Village Voice* owner Leonard N. Stern describes a family housing project in the Bronx where officials assigned all homeless families to the basement: "The huge, dimly lit, stripped-down gymnasium contained about 400 cots grouped together in family sets along the open floor. There were no lockers. Each family kept its possessions in plastic garbage bags beneath its cots." One New York City mother said, "It is very easy to get sick in a shelter or SRO because management dumps everyone into the same dorm; the young with the old, the healthy with the sickly, the thief with the honest man."

Single homeless individuals describe sleepless nights in shelters that echo with drunken nightmares, and reek with urine-soiled clothes and filthy bodies. A person lying on one cot hears and smells the sick heavings of the person on a cot six feet away. Windows and fresh air are nonexistent in a warehouse, a gymnasium, a basement, or a cubicle.

The Salvation Army's downtown shelter is the only facility in Austin, Texas, that offers free shelter, free breakfast and dinner, and shower facilities. Men and women who are willing to stand in line for an admittance ticket every day can stay for as many nights as they wish—if they abide by the short list of strict rules. Because it is almost barrier-free and it offers tolerable living conditions, this privately operated shelter fills its cots nearly every night. With city assistance, the Salvation Army opened an additional winter shelter in a vacant meatpacking warehouse. There, 240 homeless men sleep on thin mats supported by a cracked cement floor. However, except in the worst of weather, the winter shelter is rarely filled to capacity. One transient declined to sleep in it because "the conditions at the dog pound are better than in there. I ain't no animal."

Conditions at some family shelters are equally uninviting. Welfare motels and hotels rarely provide both a kitchen and a private bathroom. At their worst, welfare hotels are overcrowded, dangerous places where families cohabit a single room with rodents and roaches. At their best, public shelters are equipped with clean, private sleeping quarters for families who can close their door against noise, theft, and germs. However, families fare better in privately operated shelters that provide not only private lodging but kitchens where families can prepare their own meals and on-site services such as counseling and day care.

Sister Connie Driscoll presides over a shelter for homeless women and their children on Chicago's South Side. She asserts that all of Chicago's 5,500 shelter beds are in a safe and clean environment.

> In this city, if shelters are found to be unsafe, the Department of Human Services shuts them down and refuses to fund them. The department employs monitoring teams to make sure people in shelters are treated properly. Whenever abuses come to light, Human Services gets new people to run the facilities.

The revolving door of homelessness

Coupled with the challenge of living within the shelter system is the challenge to move out of the system and into permanent housing. Since families with children are the fastest growing segment of the homeless population, advocacy groups are especially concerned about their fate. Unfortunately, the successful transition from shelter to permanent housing is accomplished by about only half the families who become homeless. According to Homes for the Homeless, 45 percent of all homeless families in San Francisco eventually return to the shelter system. In New York City, the return-to-shelter rate is 50 percent.

Among St. Louis families surveyed, 21 percent left Salvation Army shelters to go to another shelter or into transitional housing. Another 23 percent moved from a shelter to doubled-up housing. About 53 percent found permanent

*Despite the assistance
of charities and service
providers, many
homeless families are
unable to break the
cycle of poverty and
homelessness.*

public or private rental housing. Even so, residents of St.
Louis shelters in 1985 were five times more likely to find
permanent housing than were residents in 1995.

The revolving door that leads from homelessness to independence to homelessness may hinge on the fact that
lack of shelter or affordable housing is rarely a short-term,
singular emergency such as fire or eviction. People in
emergency housing or in transitional housing typically
face a combination of economic, emotional, or health
problems that not only led to their homelessness, but may
prevent them from escaping it. In the same way that inadequate housing alone does not cause homelessness, neither
can additional shelters and affordable housing end homelessness. People without homes need help in order to solve
their varied and complex problems.

6

Help for the Homeless

IN 1994 THE CLINTON administration issued a report called *Priority: Home! The Federal Plan to End Homelessness.* The plan recommended a "continuum of care" that combined shelter, education, substance-abuse counseling, job training, and medical treatment. It also proposed $900 million in additional HUD funding to help the homeless. Designed by the Interagency Council on the Homeless, *Priority: Home!* reflected the concept that homelessness is not solely a housing issue but a complex problem requiring personalized help for each person who is homeless.

The federal government

"Continuum of care" is not a new idea within the federal government. In 1933 President Franklin D. Roosevelt launched a relief program that provided the homeless not only with shelter, but also with food, medical care, clothing, cash, and jobs. That agency, the Federal Emergency Relief Administration, worked in cooperation with the states as HUD does today. Roosevelt also launched Social Security, the Works Progress Administration, and the Civilian Conservation Corps, all federal programs that helped the disabled, the elderly, the unemployed, or the poor. The Home Owners Loan Corporation granted long-term mortgage loans at low cost to homeowners with financial difficulties, while the U.S. Housing Authority was designed to develop adequate housing throughout the nation. Thus, for more than sixty years, the federal government has tried to reduce homelessness and poverty and has tried to prevent poor people from becoming homeless.

The government, in turn, relies on citizens, whose income taxes pay for federal programs. When citizens pay their taxes, they are helping the government help the homeless. Although the cooperation between taxpayers and their government is mandatory—taxpayers must pay taxes—citizens' representatives in Congress try to plan a budget that spends tax dollars wisely. Some taxpayers favor more government spending to help the homeless. Others want to save tax dollars by reducing federal aid to the homeless. When congressional representatives debate whether or not to increase spending, reduce the federal deficit, cut welfare benefits, or add more tax dollars to a program that helps the homeless, they are debating how taxpayers' money will be spent. Similar debates are conducted in state legislatures and city budget meetings. Citizens may influence budget decisions by expressing their wishes to their representatives and by voting for representatives who support certain programs. In a nation in which government is "of the people and for the people," government help for the homeless is the result of the combined efforts of voters, taxpayers, and legislators.

Plans such as *Priority: Home!* cannot help the homeless until such plans are either funded through existing programs or legislated—accepted by Congress and the president, and signed into law. For example, HUD's secretary, Andrew Cuomo, is a longtime homeless activist who hopes to forge his ideas into policy. In response to *Priority: Home!* HUD and the Veterans Administration jointly initiated the Supported Housing partnership for homeless veterans with mental illness or substance abuse problems. However, before other new programs could be initiated, Congress voted to reduce government spending rather than increase it.

Reductions in government spending

Proposed before the U.S. Senate in 1996, the so-called balanced budget amendment was defeated by only two

President Clinton signs into law the welfare reform bill. The new legislation is aimed at moving people off the welfare rolls by transitioning them into jobs.

votes. Proponents of a balanced budget want to change the U.S. Constitution to require that the federal budget be balanced every year. Critics claim that additional cuts required to balance the budget would hurt impoverished people the most.

After the balanced budget amendment failed, the Personal Responsibility and Work Opportunity Reconciliation Act of 1996 (welfare reform) was passed by Congress and signed into law by President Clinton. This new legislation passes responsibility for the poor from federal hands into the hands of the states. It also reduces allocations that will go to each state, with cuts totaling $54 billion over six years. Every state will receive a federal grant each year, but they no longer have to provide matching funds. Although states are free to legislate and fund additional programs, they must follow new federal regulations for programs paid for with federal grants.

Beginning in 1999, recipients who receive aid can work twenty hours a week if they spend another five hours in vocational education or high school equivalency education. Since July 1, 1997, minor parents—those under eighteen—cannot receive funds unless they live with one of their parents or with another supervisory adult. To receive aid, minor parents must also attend high school or a training program as soon as their child is twelve weeks old. Because families are limited to five years of aid in a lifetime, such funds cannot be used to aid children beyond that time limit.

Welfare reform cuts $27.7 billion from the food stamp program over six years. Now homeless shelters must factor in the reduction in food stamps for homeless families, thereby adding to the expense of sheltering a homeless family. Under the new law, single, nondisabled, nonworking individuals ages eighteen to fifty can receive only three months of food stamps in a three-year period. Welfare reform also slashed SSI benefits. The Congressional Budget Office estimates that 300,000 children will be denied SSI by 2002 and 40,000 to 50,000 of these children will lose Medicaid. The Runaway and Homeless Youth program was cut by 14 percent, and the Job Training/Youth Training program by 78 percent. Reductions in these programs that help the homeless may or may not be replaced by donations from corporations and charities or by additional funding from states and local governments.

Help on the local level

After the federal government legislated welfare reform and budget cuts, charities had to determine whether they could increase funding to supplement reduced benefits to the poor and the homeless. Alexandria, Virginia, pastor David Beckman runs Bread for the World, a Christian citizens' movement against hunger. Beckman expressed his reaction to budget cuts when he said, "There's no way that churches and charities can pick up the tab for what the government is walking away from—that's clear." With families facing a lifetime limit of five years on welfare, Alexandria expects to have 300 to 400 additional, desperately poor families within its city limits by the year 2000.

Reverend Joan Campbell, general secretary of the National Council of Churches, said of welfare reform, "Everybody knew that welfare was not the answer, but the moral

goal was not ending welfare as we know it; it was ending poverty as we know it." Idealistically, moral goals are met when people view others' needs as equal to their own. In an attempt to encourage charities to help people meet the new work requirement, President Clinton suggested in March 1997 that each of the nation's churches hire at least one welfare recipient. Reverend John Steinbruck responded, "He knows better, his staff knows better and his pastor knows better." Steinbruck heads Luther Place Emergency Shelter in Washington, D.C. His skepticism stems from the fact that most churches are already short on funds and could not afford to hire additional staff. Churches are supported by financial contributions from their members. Thus, in asking churches to give more, the president asked individual members to give more. Since people who support their church typically support other charities as well, they may not be able to increase their giving. However, churches are exploring other ways to help. For example, the Greater Dallas Community of Churches hopes to recruit fifty mentoring groups, each providing one family with day care, job training, and work clothes to enable them to move from welfare to work.

Privately funded programs and local governments strive to reduce the return-to-shelter ratio in major cities, as well as prevent impoverished people from becoming homeless. New York City's Rental Assistance Program, privately funded, provides up to $200 a month per recipient for people who are leaving shelters, coming out of drug rehabilitation, or living doubled up with other people. The National Alliance to End Homelessness administers the nationwide Life Skills Program, which includes classes on budgeting and how to be a good tenant. Chicago operates telephone hot lines to prevent onetime crises from escalating into homelessness. For example, if a tenant is unable to pay rent, or if a tenant has no heat or water, he or she may turn to Chicago's hot lines for help in resolving landlord-tenant disputes.

Nonprofit organizations

In 1976 Millard Fuller founded Habitat for Humanity International on his belief that "all of God's people should have at least a simple, decent place to live." His rallying cry is "No more shacks!" Volunteers in more than 1,300 U.S. affiliates are building homes in partnership with individuals and families who move from shelters, doubled-up, or substandard housing into a Habitat house: a simple, energy-efficient home financed at no interest and paid for with owner earnings plus hundreds of work hours known as "sweat equity."

Each affiliate raises its own start-up funds. Then it selects families according to greatest need, willingness to partner, and ability to pay the $250–$300 monthly payment on a mortgage financed by the affiliate. Families' mortgage payments buy more building materials. Then Habitat families and volunteers help additional families build their homes. Thus, communities build houses and friendships as they tear down social, economic, and racial barriers.

Habitat for Humanity volunteers believe in giving "a hand up, not a handout." Therefore, each affiliate's family-nurture committee provides homeowner classes in subjects ranging from financial planning to home repair to nutrition, all geared to help each family live independently. Habitat nurtures families who have never owned an automatic washing machine or a water heater and families whose

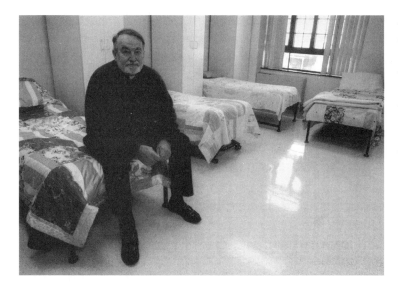

Reverend John Steinbruck sits inside the Luther Place Emergency Shelter in Washington, D.C. Steinbruck and other church leaders have criticized the government for reducing aid to the needy.

children have grown up without indoor toilets and running water. In Warren County, Virginia, Habitat's family-selection committee interviewed Paul and Ann, an older couple who reared their five adult sons in a three-room shack with no running water. "What did I do during the Blizzard of '96?" Ann laughed. "I took an ax and chopped the ice off that creek out there, and hauled the water inside the house. That's what I've done for 25 years." Now Ann and Paul are at home in a new Habitat house, while their five sons work to build a home with Pam, Damien, Ebony, and Shantel—a family that is temporarily housed in a substandard, high-rent apartment.

Due to each affiliate's careful selection process in choosing families, less than 2 percent of Habitat homeowners nationwide have had to default on their loans. When this happens, another selected family assumes the loan and joins the Habitat partnership of building homes with sweat equity. Since 1976, Habitat for Humanity International has built 60,000 homes. About 35 percent are in the United States, the rest in the world's most impoverished nations.

Roger Brown and his wife, Linda Mason, founded two nonprofit organizations that help homeless children and their parents: Bright Horizons Children's Centers, a nationwide chain of day-care centers founded in 1987, and

Horizons Initiative, founded in 1988. Michael Ryan wrote in *Parade* that by 1990 Horizons Initiative had set up eighteen play spaces at Boston homeless shelters. Shelter residents and staff expressed their gratitude along with a broader need: a full-time day-care center. In 1994 Horizons Initiative opened the Community Children's Center that now serves about seventy homeless children who range in age from two months to six years. The children's sheltered parents must attend parenting and job-skills workshops at the center, volunteer at the center, and have their children ready for the vans that pick them up at shelters around the city.

Roger Brown told Ryan, "There's already a handful of families we can look at and say, 'We've made a difference in their lives.'" One is the Latson family. Tahji Latson's two children were enrolled at the day-care center two years ago. Tahji has since rented an apartment, earned a state certificate as a preschool teacher, and plans to open her own day-care center. "Being on welfare or below the

Former president Jimmy Carter and his wife, Rosalynn (right), are among the many volunteers who help Habitat for Humanity build homes for the poor.

poverty line doesn't make you a bad mother," she says, "but it definitely erodes your self-esteem. People have to see that there is hope."

Homes for the homeless

In 1986 Leonard N. Stern founded Homes for the Homeless to offer hope to New York City's homeless mothers and children. Founded on Stern's belief that inadequate education is the root cause of homelessness, this private nonprofit group built the American Family Inns— transitional housing wherein residents receive education, job training, and services ranging from counseling to summer camps. In most traditional shelters, families must go elsewhere for such services. American Family Inns collaborate with community health care providers to provide on-site prenatal and pediatric care, dental care, immunizations, and preventive medicine. The Inns' family reunification program and two crisis nurseries are the only programs of their kind in New York State. These two programs focus on reuniting foster care children with their families and preventing foster care placement.

Other on-site family services include HER (healthy emotional relationships) workshops for victims of domestic violence, the Brownstone School after-school program, and a Jump-Start child development center for children from six months to six years old. The director of Island American Family Inn's Child Development Center says, "For most of these children, poverty and homelessness have impeded their development in nearly every area—physically, psychologically, and academically. With the Jump-Start Program we see changes in a matter of six weeks. You can't imagine what a pleasure it is to see this happen." Lewis, age nine, said proudly, "You learn more at Brownstone than in school. I used to be in the lowest reading class, now I'm in the highest."

The four American Family Inns in New York City serve over 540 families every day. Each family has a unique service plan that considers the family's individual and collective past, and its goals for the future. A caseworker helps

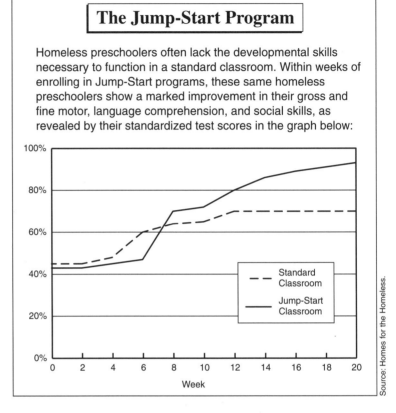

The Jump-Start Program

Homeless preschoolers often lack the developmental skills necessary to function in a standard classroom. Within weeks of enrolling in Jump-Start programs, these same homeless preschoolers show a marked improvement in their gross and fine motor, language comprehension, and social skills, as revealed by their standardized test scores in the graph below:

Standard Classroom

Jump-Start Classroom

Week

Source: Homes for the Homeless.

each parent and child within the family develop and pursue short- and long-term personal goals. Each caseworker counsels twenty families in individual weekly sessions. After a family moves into permanent housing, follow-up programs provide postplacement services for up to eighteen months. Homes for the Homeless reported in 1996 that 94 percent of all families who graduate from American Family Inns remain in permanent housing.

The program is economical. Traditional shelters expend $35 per person per day in operating costs. If a homeless family is sent to various special-use facilities, the combined daily cost per family can be as high as $270. A family of three is housed and educated at an American Family Inn for $69 per day. Overall operating costs for the American Family Inns, emergency assistance units (EAUs), and welfare hotels are about the same in New York City. However, EAUs and welfare hotels do not provide on-site programs and services. The program's creators describe the inns as "main streets of the 1990s— where all necessary services can be provided cost-effectively under one roof. Without separating the family, these Inns can foster independence and initiative—keys to family 'responsibility.'"

The program is currently funded by public and private grants and by channeling former AFDC allocations into operations costs. Local jurisdictions within New York City pay about $17 per day for each family housed in an American Family Inn. That is, for an average family of three, the government's cost for housing and on-site services is about $5.70 per person per day. Moreover, with its 94 percent success rate, return-to-shelter costs are almost eliminated, as are families' previous dependencies on low-wage jobs and diminishing welfare benefits. The program's advocates suggest that if the concept were embraced nationwide, it would benefit government, taxpayers, and homeless families alike.

The drawback to comprehensive transitional housing is that family members who participate must be willing to take responsibility for changing their lives. People who are dependent on drugs or are in abusive relationships, for instance, may or may not accept the challenge to turn away from familiar pain and difficulty in order to reshape their lives in unfamiliar ways. However, Homes for the Homeless is not designed to end chronic homelessness. Its goal is to offer hope and solutions to families who are ready for change.

Personal resources and personal friends

In addition to accepting available help, people who make the transition from homelessness to permanent housing report using personal resources such as coping skills, persistence, abilities, and faith in God or a higher power. Denise, a formerly homeless woman in the rural south, said, "I don't believe that there's no way on this earth that I could have did this without Him. God played a big role in my life." Other invaluable aids include a supportive friend or a mentor.

To mentor another person is to spend time with that person, to listen, respect, care, offer advice if asked, help if appropriate, and exhibit self-esteem and self-reliance that the mentored can emulate. Comments from formerly homeless people illustrate that even one supportive person can supply the caring and understanding that builds self-confidence. However, the homeless person must be willing to be mentored. One formerly homeless woman, Ellie, said of her shelter staff, "I wind up putting my success on the help that I got from in there, and the way they treated my kids. I could just sit back and just see how happy my kids were. And it was all coming from these people that was strangers to us. But there they was, making us so happy and giving us a new outlook on life. A new life, really a life that we had never had." Ellie's family moved from homelessness to transitional housing and then to independent living.

Youth volunteers

Independently and in groups, children and teenagers have found ways to offer aid and friendship to the homeless. In 1996, Junior Girl Scouts and Brownie troops traveled from affluent Vail, Colorado, to downtown Denver's twenty-family Salvation Army shelter. They donated clothing and toys, ate lunch with the families, helped with the dishes, and made plans to come again. In order to work shoulder-to-shoulder with homeless people, church youth groups from several mid-Atlantic states traveled to Sumter, South Carolina, to help an emergency Habitat for Humanity affiliate called Hugo Habitat build homes with twenty families whose literal shacks had been blown away by Hurricane Hugo. Teenagers and homeless adults worked together in 100° heat to clear brush, dig footers, and lay foundations, while the younger children delivered sandwiches and cold drinks to the workers. Youths in inner-city Baltimore regularly help Sandtown Habitat rehabilitate condemned row houses that become homes for the homeless. College students in more than four hundred campus chapters donate their time and building talents to Habitat when they adopt a homeless family as their home-building partners.

The homeless on the Internet: expressions of experience and hope

Advocacy organizations such as the National Coalition for the Homeless and private nonprofits such as Homes for the Homeless use the Internet to publicize their efforts to alleviate homelessness. HUD and other government agencies have long had addresses on the World Wide Web. Now the homeless themselves are sharing their opinions, experiences, and hopes in an on-line library of stories from street newspapers.

Homeless people in about twenty major cities help write and distribute street newspapers. Some publications have mentors or homeless activists who supervise the operation, serve as editors, and encourage the homeless to submit their articles, poems, and essays for inclusion in the paper. Chicago's *StreetWise* has a staff of more than a dozen and a monthly circulation of 130,000. Eugene, Oregon's *Houseless Journal* is solely produced by one homeless woman.

The Bridge School, a literacy program for low-income and homeless adults and youth in Portland, sponsors a newspaper and website called the *Burnside Cadillac.* This publication includes original contributions from Portland's homeless as well as reprinted media articles about homeless issues, a guide to resources, and ads for businesses that contribute funds to the paper and to the Bridge School. Homeless contributor Peter Statelman's poem describes the shopping carts—the Burnside Cadillacs—being pushed by the homeless near Burnside Park in Portland. On another page, rules for buying and selling papers declare that the selling price cannot exceed $1, although homeless distributors may accept private donations from buyers. Of one thousand copies published, two hundred are distributed free to the homeless people of Portland.

About twenty homeless publications have formed their own association. The 1996 North American Street

A homeless couple sells copies of Real Change, *a Seattle-based newspaper that is produced and sold by the homeless and their advocates.*

Newspaper Association includes Seattle's *Real Change,* San Francisco's *Street Sheet,* Boston's *Spare Change,* Chicago's *StreetWise,* and Charlotte's *Word on the Street. Real Change* director Timothy Harris believes that being on-line gives the *Homeless News* website "the potential to become the Associated Press of the street paper movement." That is, the words of homeless contributors from around the nation can reach a broader readership than exists in their own neighborhood, or even on their newspaper's own website. Harris writes in *Real Change,* "While most street newspapers are based in poor people's organizations that have yet to go on-line . . . plans are underway to ease these organizations onto the information highway." Thus, for the homeless and those who help them, the Internet is a tool of hope for the future.

With the aid of technological advances such as the Internet, homeless people and advocates are publicizing a national problem that has existed for more than 250 years.

From colonial times to the advent of the twenty-first century, people without homes have been a part of American society. By whatever word they are labeled—as drifters, hoboes, or the homeless—their visible, vocal, and Internet presence will continue to call for solutions to the problem of homelessness. The problem, coupled with the response of governments and housed citizens, will play a part in defining the nation's identity in the years ahead.

Organizations
to Contact

Habitat for Humanity International
Habitat and Church Streets
Americus, GA 31709
(800) HABITAT

Its U.S. affiliates are made up of community volunteers who
help low-income and homeless people build or renovate their
own homes. The organization also builds homes in impoverished nations.

Homes for the Homeless
36 Cooper Sq., 6th Floor
New York, NY 10003
(212) 529-5252

A private nonprofit organization that is the nation's largest
single provider of residential education services to homeless
families. Its American Family Inns transitional housing facilities serve homeless mothers and children in New York City.

Interagency Council on the Homeless
451 Seventh St. SW, Suite 7274
Washington, DC 20410
(202) 708-1480

Established by the Stewart B. McKinney Homeless Assistance Act of 1987, the council is made up of the heads or ap-
pointees of seventeen federal agencies for the purpose of
coordinating federal programs that assist the homeless. The
council also reports to Congress and the president on the
problem of homelessness.

National Alliance to End Homelessness
1518 K St. NW
Washington, DC 20005
(202) 638-1526

An advocacy group that seeks to form public-private partnerships among individuals, corporations, organizations, and government agencies to alleviate the causes and problems of homelessness.

National Coalition for the Homeless
1612 K St. NW, Suite 1004
Washington, DC 20006
(202) 775-1322

This advocacy group researches and distributes information on all aspects of homelessness on the national and state levels.

National Law Center on Homelessness and Poverty
918 F St. NW, Suite 412
Washington, DC 20004-1406
(202) 638-2535

A legal advocacy group that monitors and publicizes legislation affecting the homeless.

U.S. Conference of Mayors
Task Force on Hunger and Homelessness
1620 I St. NW, 4th Floor
Washington, DC 20006
(202) 293-7330

The task force studies trends in hunger and homelessness in America's major cities and the community programs that address these problems. It publishes an annual *Status Report on Hunger and Homelessness in America's Cities*.

Suggestions for Further Reading

Kevin Cwayna, *Knowing Where the Fountains Are: Stories and Stark Realities of Homeless Youth.* Minneapolis: Deaconess Press, 1993. Dr. Cwayna, founder of the Youth Housing Project in Minneapolis, examines homelessness causes, realities, and obstacles, as well as responses to the housing crisis, as experienced by older youth, with emphasis on the impact of the AIDS epidemic. Young people tell their own stories in interviews with Dr. Cwayna.

Frank Ferrell, *Trevor's Place: The Story of a Boy Who Brings Hope to the Homeless.* San Francisco: Hazelton Foundations, 1990. Chronicles the accomplishments of an eleven-year-old Philadelphia boy whose compassion for the homeless ignited a response from media, citizens, and the government, and resulted in the establishment of a homeless shelter called "Trevor's Place." This shows how one child can make a difference.

Christopher Jencks, *The Homeless.* Cambridge, MA: Harvard University Press, 1994. A well-documented, scholastic, and very readable examination of homelessness by a respected teacher and sociologist. Includes tables and extensive notes. For advanced readers.

Margaret Morton, *The Tunnel.* New Haven, CT: Yale University Press, 1995. A collection of award-winning black-and-white photographs of and interviews with underground homeless residents of New York City. Residents of the tunnel describe themselves and their daily lives in alcoves and ledges where some have lived for twenty years. For advanced readers.

Ralph da Costa Nunez, *The New Poverty: Homeless Families in America.* New York: Plenum Press, Insight Books, 1996. Dr. da Costa Nunez, president of Homes for the Homeless, has held executive-level policy positions concerning social welfare at the city and state levels of government, and he uses that background to launch the story of why Homes for the Homeless was founded and how it works. Includes numerous interviews with formerly homeless New York City mothers who now live independently and a foreword by Leonard N. Stern, founder of Homes for the Homeless.

Lisa Orr, ed., *The Homeless.* San Diego: Greenhaven Press, 1990. This anthology of excerpts from books and periodicals invites examination and comparison of authors' varying viewpoints on the subject. Each excerpt includes information about the author and provides questions to help young readers separate fact from opinion. A title in Greenhaven's Opposing Viewpoints Series.

Works Consulted

Books

Bureau of the Census, *Statistical Abstract of the United States,* 1994. Government Printing Office: Washington, DC, 1994.

Martha Burt, *Over the Edge.* New York: Russell Sage, 1992.

Lars Eighner, *Travels with Lizbeth.* New York: St. Martin's Press, 1993.

Robert Famighetti, ed., *World Almanac and Book of Facts 1996.* Mahwah, NJ: World Almanac Books, 1996.

Millard Fuller with Diane Scott, *No More Shacks! The Daring Vision of Habitat for Humanity.* Waco, TX: Word Books, 1986.

Jonathan Kozol, *Rachel and Her Children: Homeless Families in America.* New York: Crown, 1988.

Jamshid A. Momeni, ed., *Homelessness in the United States.* Vol. 1, *State Surveys.* New York: Greenwood Press, 1989.

Marjorie J. Robertson and Milton Greenblatt, eds., *Homelessness: A National Perspective.* New York: Plenum Press, 1992.

Peter Rossi, *Down and Out in America.* Chicago: University of Chicago Press, 1989.

David A. Snow and Leon Anderson, *Down on Their Luck.* Berkeley: University of California Press, 1993.

Doug A. Timmer, D. Stanley Eitzen, and Kathryn D. Talley, *Paths to Homelessness: Extreme Poverty and the Urban Housing Crisis.* Boulder, CO: Westview Press, 1994.

Jennifer Wolch and Michael Dear, *Malign Neglect.* San Francisco: Jossey-Bass Publishers,1993.

Periodicals

Jonathan Alter, "A Real Piece of Work," *Newsweek,* August 25, 1997.

Angela Ards, "To Be Young, Female & Black," *Village Voice,* February 13, 1996.

Associated Press, "Bitterly Cold Weather Worries Va. Homeless Advocates," *Northern Virginia Daily,* January 18, 1997.

Associated Press, "Gingrich: Clinton Hurting Welfare Reform," *Northern Virginia Daily,* May 31, 1997.

Associated Press, "Praying for an Answer," *Northern Virginia Daily,* March 8, 1997.

"Bishop Calls Camping Ban 'Cruel,'" *National Catholic Reporter,* March 1, 1996.

Burnside Cadillac, vol. 2, no. 3, August 1996, www.teleport.com/~bcad.

Children's Defense Fund, "Summary of Legislation Affecting Children in 1996," November 22, 1996, www.tmn.com.cdf.

Children's Defense Fund, "Summary of the New Welfare Legislation," October 23, 1996, www.tmn.com/cdf.

Adam Cohen, "The Great American Welfare Lab," *Time,* April 21, 1997, pp. 74–76.

Jed Dillingham, "UK Professor Is Attempting to Heal Wounds of Homelessness," *Dawson Springs Progress,* December 23, 1996.

Timothy Harris, "Good News from Chicago," *RealChange: Seattle's Homeless Newspaper,* December 22, 1996, www.rchange@speakeasy.org.

Diane Hoffbauer and Maureen Prenn, "A Place to Call One's Own: Choosing Books About Homelessness," *Social Education,* vol. 60, no. 3, March 1996.

Homes for the Homeless, "A Tale of Two Nations: The Creation of American 'Poverty Nomads,'" December 21, 1996, hn4061@handsnet.org.

Homes for the Homeless, "Facts About Homeless Children and Families," December 21, 1996, hn4061@handsnet.org.

Elizabeth W. Lindsey, "Mothers' Perceptions of Factors Influencing the Restabilization of Homeless Families," *Families in Society: The Journal of Contemporary Human Services,* 1996.

Rob McCallum, "Girl Scouts Learn About, Help Denver's Homeless," *Vail Daily Newspaper,* www.colorado.net.

John McCormick and Evan Thomas, "One Family's Journey from Welfare to Work," *Newsweek,* May 26, 1997.

"More Pressures on the Homeless," *America,* April 13, 1996.

National Coalition for the Homeless, 1996 and 1997 Fact Sheets, nci.ari.net.

Cynthia Rocha, Alice K. Johnson, Kay Young McChesney, and William H. Butterfield, "Predictors of Permanent Housing for Sheltered Homeless Families," *Families in Society: The Journal of Contemporary Human Services,* January 1996.

Michael Ryan, "Here, Every Child Is Cared For," *Parade,* September 21, 1997.

Robert J. Samuelson, "The Culture of Poverty," *Newsweek,* May 5, 1997.

Janet Schrader, "Lost on the Road to Reform," *Washington Post,* May 11, 1997.

Sandra Stencel, ed., "Helping the Homeless," *CQ Researcher,* January 26, 1996.

Kevin J. Swick, "Teacher Strategies for Supporting Homeless Students and Families," *Clearing House,* May/June 1996.

Guy Trebay, "Notice of Dispossess," *Village Voice,* January 16, 1996.

James Wilworth, "This Is Your Father's Life," *Time,* April 14, 1997.

Niki L. Young, "There's No Place Like Home: An Analysis of Homeless Testimonial Narratives," *Midwest Quarterly,* vol. 37, no. 3, Spring 1996.

Index

Picture Credits

Cover Photo: © Mark Ludak/Impact Visuals

© Mark E. Ahlstrom, 31

Archive Photos, 41

AP/Wide World Photos, 12, 42, 49, 91

© David Bacon/Impact Visuals, 39

© Neal Boenzi/Archive Photos, 7

© George Cohen/Impact Visuals, 84

© Harvey Finkle/Impact Visuals, 60, 62, 75, 80

© Andrew Fremont-Smith/Impact Visuals, 18

© Jerome Friar/Impact Visuals, 17

© Terry Gydesen/Imact Visuals, 72

© Marilyn Humphries/Impact Visuals, 14

© Andrew Lichenstein/Impact Visuals, 57, 76

© Tom McKitterick/Impact Visuals, 51, 76

Reuters/Stephen Jaffe/Archive Photos, 87

Reuters/Bruce Young/Archive Photos, 64

© Theodore E. Roseen, 79

© Stacy Rosenstock/Impact Visuals, 27

© Dana Schuerholz/Impact Visuals, 98

UPI/Corbis-Bettmann, 55, 92

© Teun Voeten/Impact Visuals, 45, 52

© Ruby Washington/Archive Photos, 28

© Jim West/Impact Visuals, 68

About the Author

Sara Dixon Criswell is the founder and former president of Warren County Habitat for Humanity in Virginia. As an advocate for low-income housing, and as a writer for children, she is a frequent guest speaker at civic and service organizations and elementary schools. She assists disaster victims through her work at the Federal Emergency Management Agency's Mount Weather Emergency Assistance Center.

A former middle school and elementary school librarian, she writes primarily for publishers of educational materials. Her textbook, *Virginia,* reflects her lifelong interest in Virginia history and geography. She and her three cats live in Virginia's Blue Ridge Mountains.